SOCIAL SCIENCES,

CONCEPTS OF BRANCHES AND RELATIONSHIPS

ISBN: 978-1-291-52321-8

I0425525

Andreas Sofroniou   2013 ©   Copyright

Andreas Sofroniou   2013 ©   Copyright

SOCIAL SCIENCES,

CONCEPTS OF BRANCHES AND RELATIONSHIPS

ISBN: 978-1-291-52321-8

CONTENTS

Page

1. SOCIETY AND SOCIAL RELATIONSHIPS

1.1 Human society

Social sciences consist of branches pertaining to the study of human society and social relationships. The disciplines usually encompassed, at least in some of their aspects, are: anthropology, demography, economics, geography, political science, psychology, sociology and philosophy.

Also frequently included are those areas of education that deal with the social contexts of learning and the relation of the school to the social order.

History is regarded by many as a social science, and certain areas of historical study are almost indistinguishable from work done in the social sciences. Most historians, however, consider history as one of the humanities. It is generally best, in any case, to consider history as marginal to the humanities and social sciences, since its insights and techniques pervade both.

The study of comparative law may also be regarded as a part of the social sciences, although it is ordinarily pursued in schools of law rather than in departments or schools containing most of the other social sciences.

1.2 Behavioural science

Since the 1950s the term behavioural sciences has often been applied to the disciplines designated as the social sciences. Those who favour this term do so in part because these disciplines are thus brought closer to some of the sciences, such as physical anthropology and physiological psychology, which also deal with human behaviour.

Whether the term behavioural sciences will in time supplant "social sciences" or whether it will, as neologisms so often have before, fade away is impossible to say. For the purposes of this article, the two terms may be considered synonymous.

Early approaches often sought to adapt to social enquiry the methods used to investigate the natural world. Laws were postulated and evidence for them sought. This approach has been called naturalism or positivism.

Such methods and views persist to the present day, and some social scientists share objectives with natural scientists. They seek to test hypotheses and to explain and predict phenomena. They use experiments and statistical techniques to establish correlations. Economists and psychologists are frequently to be found in this group.

1.3 Codification of sciences

The codification of the social sciences began in the 18th century, when the success of the natural sciences inspired the belief that humanity could be investigated similarly.

However, from the late 19th century many writers, among them, most notably, the German sociologist Weber, maintained that the social sciences could still be rigorous without copying the methods of natural science. Rather than looking for law-like statements or working numerically, the social scientist could be more interpretive and intuitive.

Social scientists following this approach tend to lay greater stress on the observation and interpretation of complex phenomena as they occur in the world rather than in experiments, and on eliciting the views of those being studied. Anthropologists and sociologists are frequently to be found in this group.

1.4 Combination of approaches

While the quantitative and qualitative approaches have different antecedents and are used for different purposes, the understanding of a phenomenon or problem often requires a combination.

For example, attempts to understand, ameliorate, and prevent famines in Africa require the skills not only of economists, who analyse the effects of fluctuations in commodity prices on the ability of nations to import foodstuffs, but also of anthropologists, who investigate the ways in which farmers themselves husband their resources in a drought, thus helping aid agencies to formulate appropriate strategies.

Social scientists are found in almost every society in the world, as their work is used by governments and public and private bodies in the attempt not only to understand the world, but to master it. It is increasingly recognized that the great challenges of over-population, environmental degradation, economic revival in the former Eastern bloc and Africa, and the spread of Aids cannot be met by technical or technological solutions alone. It is necessary to understand why people act as they do and to analyse the interaction of a multiplicity of forces.

However, disagreements among social scientists in their analyses of issues and in their proposals for action, and their increasing specialization, mean that the policy-maker wishing to use social science research findings is faced with a formidable task.

2. SCIENTIFIC DIVISIONS

2.1 Anthropology

Anthropology, as the study of humanity, is divided into two main areas of interest: the physical structure and evolution of mankind, and the social organizations and cultural systems of human groups.

In the 19th century, anthropology was concerned with theories of both physical and social evolution, so-called 'primitive' people being regarded as representative of earlier stages of mankind. Both physical and social differences were considered together in theories of race.

In the early 20th century, the study of social and cultural differences became a separate discipline, known as social anthropology in the UK and cultural anthropology in the USA. At the same time, anthropologists started to become more involved in fieldwork research.

Early anthropologists like Frazer had had little or no experience of the different societies they were writing about, but Malinowski was one of the first anthropologists to observe a society by living with the people, studying their language as well as their cultural system, and writing about them in an ethnography, an analysis based on such fieldwork.

In the USA, cultural anthropology traces its origins to Franz Boas (1858-1942), who studied various North-west Indian groups, and whose many notable students included Mead. Until World War II, most anthropological studies were of 'primitive' people, usually in European colonies, and the dominant theoretical influence in the UK was functionalism.

After World War II, more studies began to be carried out in societies with long traditions of written history in Europe and Asia, and new theoretical approaches, such as the structuralism of Levi-Strauss, appeared. Modern anthropologists study people in all settings, from industrial cities to remote rain forests.

By living within a society and participating in its activities, learning its language, and observing its daily life, the anthropologist builds up knowledge of that society's kinship system, social organization, culture, law, rituals, and myths. By comparing this cultural system with others, the anthropologist attempts to understand the variety of human social experience as much as possible through the eyes of different people all over the world.

2.2 Demography

Demography is the systematic study of human populations, addressed primarily to their growth, size, and structure. The main sources of data are the census and vital statistics, which developed in the 19th century. In the 20th century, population studies have developed in two main directions.

Formal demography is concerned with abstract population mathematics. It shows how rates of birth, fertility, mortality, marriage, and migration combine to produce different population structures, densities, and distributions. Social demography relates this abstract study to the economics and culture of particular societies in different times and places, in order to determine the causes and influence of changing population trends.

Sustained declines in fertility and death rates (see demographic transition) have had major implications for social policy in modern societies; demographers project population changes to assist in the planning of schooling, transport, health, and other services.

2.3 Economics

From the mid-16th century to the final quarter of the 20th century, economic thought can be split into five main historical schools:

- mercantilism;

- the economics of the French physiocrats;

- classical (and neoclassical) economics;

- Keynesianism; and

- monetarism.

The schools overlap, and they represent broad categories of thought which do not necessarily encompass the views of all economists.

The mercantilists, between the mid-16th and mid-18th centuries, argued that the wealth of nations depended on their balance of trade. With the simple monetary system that existed, proponents of the theory were concerned to maximize the amount of precious metals in the country. Protectionism was encouraged.

Classical critics of mercantilism, beginning with the philosopher Hume, demonstrated that attempts to accumulate bullion were likely to prove self-defeating, because inflows of gold would raise domestic price levels to the point of making domestic producers uncompetitive, therefore causing gold to flow out again as more imports were bought.

The French physiocrats of the 18th century, led by Francois Quesnay (1694-1774), accorded pre-eminence to the agricultural sector, which they saw as the only source of wealth, and also the source of tax revenue. They believed in the role of government being limited to preserving the natural order. They also believed in free trade. Thus their approach was *laissez-faire*.

The physiocrats' ideas of *laissez-faire* and free trade were adopted by the classical economists. Much of modern micro-economics stems from the theories of classical economics, centring on Smith's *Wealth of Nations* (1776). The marginal analysis of the 19th century led to the development of neo-classical economics as a refinement and progression from classical economics.

It clarified the mode of interaction of supply and demand through the price mechanism, and resolved a number of problems that had troubled classical economic theory, for example the apparent paradox that diamonds (an inessential luxury) are usually more 'valuable' than water (a necessity of life).

The principal contributors to classical and then neo-classical economics include, in chronological order: Smith, Robert Malthus (1766-1834), Ricardo, Mill, William Stanley Jevons (1835-82), Marshall, Arthur Cecil Pigou (1877-1959), Walras, Pareto, and Francis Ysidro Edgeworth (1845-1926). The central tenet in classical economics is that of competition.

The law of supply and demand ensures that the price of a good balances supply and demand. Competitive markets ensure that the self-seeking behaviour of individuals results in efficient, socially optimal allocation of resources and production. This is Adam Smith's 'invisible hand'. The role of government is limited to intervention in cases where a market does not exist or works imperfectly.

In the early part of the 20th century, economists argued over the role of government in controlling unemployment caused by fluctuations in demand. Those in the classical tradition argued that government should maintain a balanced budget; others argued for government expenditure financed by budget deficits. The issue was resolved by

Keynes in 1936 in *The General Theory of Employment, Interest and Money*. This work laid the foundation of what is now called macro-economics.

Keynesianism favours demand management by government through the use of both fiscal and monetary policy. Monetarism, prominent in the 1970s and 1980s, represented resurgence and updating of pre-Keynesian thought on macro-economic issues.

It stressed the importance of the money supply as the means of controlling aggregate money demand and inflation but rejected the notion that either monetary or fiscal policy could exercise any lasting influence on the level of output and employment: the money supply, it was argued, determined only the price level, not the volume of output and employment.

2.4 Geography

Human geography is the study and body of knowledge concerning the relationship between the earth's surface and the people who live on it. Karl Ritter (1779-1859), the founder of modern human geography, emphasized the influence of the natural environment on human activity and development.

Subsequently human geographers tended to concern themselves primarily with the uniqueness of particular peoples and regions. Since the 1950s more effort has gone into discovering the universal laws that may govern human behaviour and organization over the surface of the planet.

There has been a fragmentation of study into fields such as industrial, urban, agricultural, transport, and political geography, demography, and ecology.

For some, human geography has become a spatial science, involving locational analysis of the proximity and distribution of centres of human activity. Mathematical modelling often plays an important part in such work. Another trend, often seen as conflicting, has been to study the distribution of wealth, resources, and the provision of education and health services.

There is an increasing understanding that present human geography cannot be understood without reference to the past, through the field of historical geography. Mental maps are now compiled to record individuals' experience of spatial patterns, as opposed to the actual distribution of human activity. Ethnic group, social class, and gender are all factors that are increasingly taken into account.

2.5 Politics

Politics is the study and practice of government and the exercise of authority. Efforts are made to influence, gain, or wield power at various levels of government, internally and internationally, rather than in private settings and associations.

Modes of political activity are highly diverse, varying from dispute resolution and formal elections to the threat or use of outright coercion or force.

The degree to which people can engage in political activity also varies in different countries: in open societies, individuals have more freedom to participate in the exercise of political power than in closed societies, where such power is restricted to small groups.

2.6 Psychology

Psychology is 'the science of mental life', in the words of James, one of its great figures. Psychology concerns both the normal and abnormal workings of the mind, whereas psychiatry only deals with the latter.

The earliest scientific psychology was the study in the 19th century of sensory perception. This and other major psychological problems were defined earlier by the philosophers Locke and Hume, who theorized about emotion, motivation, sensation, memory, and understanding.

The first psychology courses were established in the 1870s by Wundt at Leipzig and James at Harvard. Experimental method and the development of statistical tests have been crucial to psychology's advance. But major discoveries have been made through more informal work, such as the conversational studies of children's reasoning by Piaget.

In Austria, Freud created psychoanalysis in the course of treating neurosis, but turned it into a general theory of personality, motivation, child development, and mental illness.

A recurrent question in behaviour genetics is the relative impact of heredity and experience, particularly very early experience. Galton introduced modern methods for investigating this, still a dominant issue in studies of sex differences and of intelligence and personality.

Progress in mid-20th-century psychology centred on learning theories, especially those of behaviourism, associated with Watson, and Skinner. These derived general laws of learning from animal experiments on the control of behaviour through conditioning. This work has had important applications in clinical psychology and the treatment of psychiatric illness.

However, in the 1950s behaviourism's oversimplified conceptual base and sacrifice of realism to experimental rigour came to seem increasingly inadequate. This was one reason for the rise of humanistic psychology.

Technological advances are helping to overcome these problems: it is now possible to record the activities of the brain in various ways; knowledge of genetics has increased dramatically; and computers assist in statistical analysis.

Computers have also provided a reference point for cognitive psychology, which since World War II has become the dominant area of research. It grew out of work on memory and problem-solving, and from the analogy with computers. It concerns itself with just those kinds of questions for which behaviourism appeared manifestly inadequate: language development, and the nature and development of human thought and knowledge.

Cognitive psychology shares its ancestry in German Gestalt psychology with modern social psychology, the other major development since World War II. Social psychology addresses such topics as prejudice, relationships, and misunderstandings of ourselves and others. It has also been influenced by ethology. Psychology finds application in industry, advertising, education, child-rearing, and, through clinical psychology, in the diagnosis and treatment of psychiatric illness.

2.7 Sociology

Sociology deals with the systematic study of the development, structure, and functioning of society. The late 19th-century writings of Marx, Weber, and Durkheim laid the foundations of sociology. All three analysed many facets of their own societies, in the more general context of observing the causes and consequences of the transition from traditional pre-industrial life to modern societies.

The fundamental postulate of sociology is that human beings act not by their own free decisions taken rationally, but under the influence of history and culture, and the expectations and demands of others: human beings are both the products and the makers of their societies.

Sociologists are less concerned with the characteristics of individuals than with patterns of behaviour (between doctors and patients, for instance, or priests and parishioners), which recur irrespective of the individuals involved. During the 20th century, sociologists have been particularly interested in the influence of role, status, class, and power on experience and behaviour, in the family and in the community; in the factors which contribute to cohesion and conflict; in social structure and social stratification; and in social problems such as crime, drug addiction, and domestic violence.

There are many approaches to sociology, from the functionalism of Parsons to the Marxism of the Frankfurt School. While some sociologists are primarily theorists, many analyse data gathered through interviews, observation, and surveys. Sociological findings are used increasingly by governments and businesses such as advertising and public relations.

3. PHILOSOPHY OF SCIENCE

3.1 Naturalism

Naturalism (in philosophy), is an outlook which stresses the role of facts about human nature in explaining human thought, and, more generally, sees human beings firmly as parts of the natural order.

Naturalism is broadly opposed to religious and metaphysical outlooks. Thus naturalism is frequently (although not necessarily) associated with materialism and a high estimation of the physical sciences.

Naturalist theories have both an explanatory and a justificatory aspect. They seek in the first instance to show that it is possible to explain why we think the way we do in terms of facts about our natural constitution; and they then seek to show that by appealing to those facts it is possible to provide as much of a justification for our ways of thinking as can reasonably be demanded.

There are important strains of naturalism in the philosophies of Hume and Wittgenstein. Ethical naturalism regards moral judgements as grounded in, and perhaps even as deducible from, facts about human nature.

3.2 Concepts and methods

The investigation of the concepts and methods of the natural and the scientific subjects started with philosophy in ancient Greece, when metaphysicians were formalising the method of questioning.

In the fifteenth an sixteenth centuries, there were two major themes. Historically the most important is the realism debate which dates back to the time of the pioneer astronomer scientists Galileo (1564-1642) and Copernicus (1473-1543) and is concerned with the interpretation of scientific theories.

The question is whether these theories should be regarded as true descriptions of the world (scientific realism) or whether they are rather instruments which are not literally true, but simply useful in that they enable us to make successful predictions about immediately observable phenomena (instrumentalism).

3.3 Rationality

A more recent debate concerning the nature of scientific progress is the rationality debate, which asks how we can characterize the 'scientific method', or even whether such a single, universal method can be identified. Both debates have strong links with epistemology, the theory of knowledge.

On the question of scientific rationality we can ask what sort of justification there can be for the choice of one scientific theory over another. And in the realism issue, we can ask whether we have adequate justification for regarding scientific statements as literally true.

A further question is the relationship between the natural sciences (such as physics and chemistry) and the social sciences (such as economics and sociology). Should they be regarded as close enough to share the same methods (as in Comte's positivism)? Or are the methods of the natural sciences inappropriate for the subject-matter of the social sciences? Do the natural and social sciences even have the same aim?

It has been argued that the aim of natural science is prediction and control of natural processes, whereas the aim of the social sciences is to understand human behaviour.

The question of reductionism plays a role here: can sociology be reduced to psychology, and psychology in turn to a more physically grounded neuroscience? Or are social and psychological processes irreducible?

3.4 Reductionism

Reductionism is the claim that philosophically problematic notions can be adequately explained by appeal to more basic ones. The claim that a notion is problematic is, of course, relative to a philosophical position.

Hence empiricist philosophers have sometimes tried to reduce notions of which we can have no sense-experience to those that we do. On a larger scale, physicalism is the claim that, ultimately, all scientific explanations can be given in terms of theoretical physics.

3.5 Correlation

Correlation (in statistics) refers to the interdependence of sets of data. The correlation coefficient measures in some sense the similarity between two scores, independently of the units in which the data is presented. The coefficient is usually a number between -1 and +1. Positive values imply that as one score increases so does the other, negative coefficients indicate a decrease in one score compared with an increase in the other.

Coefficients of -1 and +1 are said to exhibit perfect negative or positive correlation. A zero value indicates no correlation, although it does not imply that the data sets are necessarily independent.

Similarly, positive correlation does not guarantee a casual connection. Two factors may be linked coincidentally or a third factor may be at work. For instance, the increase in fat consumption may have coincided with an increase in cigarette smoking and it may be this which has affected the incidence of heart attacks.

Detecting and explaining correlations are prime tasks for researchers in social sciences such as psychology and economics.

4. ORIGIN AND FUTURE OF SOCIAL SCIENCES

4.1 Fundament1al ideas

Although, strictly speaking, the social sciences do not precede the 19th century--that is, as distinct and recognized disciplines of thought--one must go back farther in time for the origins of some of their fundamental ideas and objectives.

In the largest sense, the origins go all the way back to the ancient Greeks and their rationalist inquiries into the nature of man, state, and morality. The heritage of both Greece and Rome is a powerful one in the history of social thought as it is in so many other areas of Western society.

Very probably, apart from the initial Greek determination to study all things in the spirit of dispassionate and rational inquiry, there would be no social sciences today. True, there have been long periods of time, as during the Western Middle Ages, when the Greek rationalist temper was lacking.

But the recovery of this temper, through texts of the great classical philosophers, is the very essence of the Renaissance and the Age of Reason in modern European history. With the Age of Reason, in the 17th and 18th centuries, one may begin.

4.2 Behavioural science

Behavioural science is any of various disciplines dealing with the subject of human actions, usually including the fields of sociology, social and cultural anthropology, psychology, and behavioural aspects of biology, economics, geography, law, psychiatry, and political science.

The term gained currency in the 1950s in the United States; it is often used synonymously with "social sciences," although some writers distinguish between them. The term behavioural sciences suggests an approach that is more experimental than that connoted by the older term social sciences.

4.3 Future of social sciences

What has been covered in the preceding paragraphs may be the most that can be said within restricted compass about the social sciences of the 2ist century without turning to the individual social sciences themselves and related disciplines.

The concern here has been with only those major contextual influences, tendencies of overall character, and dominant ideas or theories that the social sciences taken as a whole manifest in one degree or other.

There is one final aspect of the subject that must be considered briefly, for how it is resolved will have much effect upon the future of the social sciences in the West. This is the relation of the social sciences to organized society, to government and industry, and other institutional centres of authority.

At the present time, there is a significant and undoubtedly growing feeling among social scientists, especially younger ones, that the relationship has become altogether too close. The social sciences, it is said, must maintain their distance, their freedom, from bureaucratized government and industry. Otherwise they will lose their inherent powers of honest and dispassionate criticism of the ineffective or evil in society.

Although there may be a certain amount of feeling ranging from the naïve to the politically revolutionary in such sentiments, they cannot be taken lightly, as is apparent from the serious consideration that is being given on a steadily rising scale to the whole problem of the relationship between social science and social policy.

Since the inception of the social sciences--since, indeed, the time when the universities in the West came into being for the express purpose of training professional men in law, theology, and medicine--man has properly sought, through knowledge, to influence social policy, taking this latter term in the widest sense to include not merely the policies of national government but of local government, business, professions, and so on.

What else, it may be asked, are the social sciences all about if it is not to use knowledge to improve social life; and how else but through influencing of the major institutions can such improvement take place?

So much is true, comes the answering response. But in the process of seeking to influence the great agencies of modern power and function-- of what is loosely called the Establishment--the social sciences may themselves become influenced adversely by the values of power and affluence to be found in these great agencies. They themselves may become identified with the status quo. What the social sciences should give, say the partisans of this view, is a continuation of the revolutionary or at least profoundly reformist tradition that was begun in the 18th century by the philosophers of reason who, detesting the official establishment of their day, sought on their own to transform it.

What is today called objectivity or methodological rigour turns out to be, say these same partisans, acceptance of the basic values of reigning government and industry.

It is this essential conflict regarding the purposes of the social sciences, the relation of the social sciences to government and society, and the role of the individual social scientist in the society of the 20th century that bids fair at this moment to be the major conflict of the years ahead. How it is resolved may very well determine the fate of the social sciences, now less than two centuries old.

4.4 Specializations

A major point to make about the social sciences of the 2ist century is the vast increase in the number of social scientists involved, in the number of academic and other centres of teaching and research in the social sciences, and in their degree of both comprehensiveness and specialization.

The explosion of the sciences generally in the 2ist century--an explosion responsible for the fact that a majority of all scientists who have ever lived in human history are now alive--has had, as one of its signal elements, the explosion of the social sciences. Not only has there been development and proliferation but there has also been a spectacular diffusion of the social sciences.

Beginning in a few places in western Europe and the United States in the 19th century, the social sciences, as bodies of ongoing research and centres of teaching, are today to be found almost everywhere in the world. In considerable part this has followed the spread of universities from the West to other parts of the world and, within universities, the very definite shift away from the hegemony once held by humanities alone to the near-hegemony held today by the sciences, physical and social.

Specialization has been as notable a tendency in the social sciences as in the biological and physical sciences. This is reflected not only in varieties of research but also in course offerings in academic departments. Whereas not very many years ago, a couple of dozen advanced courses in a social science reflected the specialization and diversity of the discipline even in major universities with graduate schools, today a hundred such courses are found to be not enough.

Side by side with this strong trend toward specialization, however, is another, countering trend: that of cross-fertilization and interdisciplinary cooperation. At the beginning of the century, down in fact until World War II, the several disciplines existed each in a kind of splendid isolation from the others.

That historians and sociologists, for example, might ever work together in curricula and research projects would have been scarcely conceivable prior to about 1945. Each social science tended to follow the course that emerged in the 19th century: to be confined to a single, distinguishable, if artificial, area of social reality.

4.5 Cross-disciplinary work

Today, evidences are all around of cross-disciplinary work and of fusion within a single social science of elements drawn from other social sciences. Thus, there are such vital areas of work as political sociology, economic anthropology, psychology of voting, and industrial sociology. Single concepts such as "structure," "function," "alienation," and "motivation" can be seen employed variously to useful effect in several social sciences.

The techniques of one social science can be seen consciously incorporated into another or into several social sciences. If history has provided much in the way of perspective to sociology or anthropology, each of these two has provided perspective, and also whole techniques, such as statistics and survey, to history.

In short, specialization is by no means without some degree at least of countertendencies such as fusion and synthesis.

Another outstanding characteristic of each of the social sciences in the 21st century is its professionalization. Without exception, the social sciences have become bodies of not merely research and teaching but also practice, in the sense that this word has in medicine or engineering.

Down until about World War II, it was a rare sociologist or political scientist or anthropologist who was not a holder of academic position. There were economists and psychologists to be found in banks, industries, government, even in private consultantship, but the numbers were relatively tiny.

Overwhelmingly the social sciences had visibility alone as academic disciplines, concerned essentially with teaching and with more or less basic, individual research. All this has changed profoundly, and on a vast scale, during the past three decades.

Today there are as many economists and psychologists outside academic departments as within, if not more. The number of sociologists, political scientists, and demographers to be found in government, industry, and private practice rises constantly. Equally important is the changed conception or image of the social sciences.

Today, to a degree unknown before World War II, the social sciences are conceived as policy-making disciplines, concerned with matters of national welfare in their professional capacities in just as sure a sense as any of the physical sciences. Inevitably, tensions have arisen within the social sciences as the result of processes of professionalization.

Those persons who are primarily academic can all too easily feel that those who are primarily professional have different and competing identifications of themselves and their disciplines.

4. 6 Nature of the research

The emphasis upon research in the social sciences has become almost transcending within recent decades. This situation is not at all different from that which prevails in the physical sciences and the professions in this age. Prior to about 1945, the functions of teaching and research had approximately equal value in many universities and colleges.

The idea of a social (or physical) scientist appointed to an academic institution for research alone, or with research preponderant, was scarcely known. Research bureaus and institutes in the social sciences were very few and did not rival traditional academic departments and colleges as prestige-bearing entities.

All of that was changed decisively beginning with the period just after World War II. From governments and foundations, large sums of money passed into the universities--usually not to the universities as such, but rather to individuals or small groups of individuals, each eminent for research. Research became the uppermost value in the social sciences (as in the physical) and hence, of course, in the universities themselves.

4.7 Mathematical and quantitative methods

Probably the greatest single change in the social sciences during the past generation has been the widespread introduction of mathematical and other quantitative methods. Without question, economics is the discipline in which the most spectacular changes of this kind have taken place.

So great is the dominance of mathematical techniques here--resulting in the eruption of what is called econometrics to a commanding position in the discipline--that, to the outsider, economics today almost appears to be a branch of mathematics. But in sociology, political science, social psychology, and anthropology, the impact of quantitative methods, above all, of statistics, has also been notable.

No longer does statistics stand alone, a separate discipline, as it did in effect during the 19th century. This area today is inseparable from each of the social sciences, though, in the field of mathematics, statistics still remains eminently distinguishable, the focus of highly specialized research and theory.

4.8 Technological influences

Within the past decade or two, the use of computers and of the entire complex techniques associated with computers has become a staple of social-science research and teaching. Through the data storage and data retrieval of electronic computers, working with amounts and diversity of data that would call for the combined efforts of hundreds, even thousands of technicians, the social sciences have been able to deal with both the extensive and intensive aspects of human behaviour in ways that would once have been inconceivable.

The so-called computer revolution in modern thought has been, in short, as vivid a phase of the social as the physical sciences, not to mention other areas of modern life. The problem as it is stated by mature social scientists is to use computers in ways in which they are best fitted but without falling into the fallacy that they can alone guide, direct, and supply vital perspective in the study of man.

Closely related to mathematical, computer, and other quantitative aspects of the social sciences is the vast increase in the empiricism of modern social science. Never in history has so much in the way of data been collected, examined, classified, and brought to the uses of social theory and social policy alike.

What has been called the triumph of the fact is nowhere more visible than in the social sciences. Without question, this massive empiricism has been valuable, indispensable indeed, to those seeking explanations of social structures and processes.

Empiricism, however, like quantitative method, is not enough in itself. Unless related to hypothesis, theory, or conclusion, it is sterile, and most of the leading social scientists of today reflect this view in their works. Too many, however, deal with the gathering and classifying of data as though these were themselves sufficient.

It is the quest for data, for detailed, factual knowledge of human beliefs, opinions, and attitudes, as well as patterns and styles of life-- familial, occupational, political, religious, and so on--that has made the use of surveys and polls another of the major tendencies in the social sciences of this century. The poll data one sees in his newspaper are hardly more than the exposed portion of an iceberg.

Literally thousands of polls, questionnaires, and surveys are going on at any given moment today in the social sciences. The survey or polling method ranks with the quantitative indeed in popularity in the social sciences, both being, obviously, indispensable tools of the empiricism just mentioned.

4.9 Social statistics and geography

Two final manifestations of the social sciences in the 19th century are social statistics and social (or human) geography. At that time, neither achieved the notability and acceptance in colleges and universities that such fields as political science and economics did.

Both, however, were as clearly visible by the latter part of the 20th century as any of the other social sciences. And both were to exert a great deal of influence on the other social sciences by the beginning of the 21st century: social statistics on sociology and social psychology pre-eminently; social geography on political science, economics, history, and certain areas of anthropology, especially those areas dealing with the dispersion of races and the diffusion of cultural elements.

In social statistics the key figure of the century was a Belgian, Adolphe Quetelet, who was the first, on any systematic basis, to call attention to the kinds of structured behaviour that could be observed and identified only through statistical means. It was Quetelet who brought into prominence the momentous concept of "the average man" and his behaviour.

The two major figures in social or human geography in the century were Friedrich Ratzel in Germany and Paul Vidal de la Blache in France. Both broke completely with the crude environmentalism of earlier centuries, which had sought to show how topography and climate actually determine human behaviour, and they substituted the more subtle and sophisticated insights into the relationships of land, sea, and climate on the one hand and, on the other, the varied types of culture and human association that are to be found on earth.

In summary, by the end of the 19th century all the major social sciences had achieved a distinctiveness, an importance widely recognized, and were, especially in the cases of economics and political science, fully accepted as disciplines in the universities. Most important, they were generally accepted as sciences in their own right rather than as minions of philosophy.

5. DEVELOPMENT OF THE SEPARATE DISCIPLINES

5.1 Unification and specialisation

Among the disciplines that formed the social sciences, two contrary, for a time equally powerful, tendencies at first dominated them. The first was the drive toward unification, toward a single, master social science, whatever it might be called. The second tendency was toward specialization of the individual social sciences.

If, clearly, it is the second that has triumphed, with the results to be seen in the disparate, sometimes jealous, highly specialized disciplines seen today, the first was not without great importance and must also be examined.

What emerges from the critical rationalism of the 18th century is not, in the first instance, a conception of need for a plurality of social sciences, but rather for a single science of society that would take its place in the hierarchy of the sciences that included the fields of astronomy, physics, chemistry, and biology.

When, in the 1820s, Comte wrote calling for a new science, one with man the social animal as the subject, he assuredly had but a single, encompassing science of society in mind--not a congeries of disciplines, each concerned with some single aspect of man's behaviour in society.

The same was true of Bentham, Marx, and Spencer. All these minds, and there were many others to join them, saw the study of society as a unified enterprise. They would have scoffed, and on occasion did, at any notion of a separate economics, political science, sociology, and so on. Society is an indivisible thing, they would have argued; so, too, must be the study of society.

It was, however, the opposite tendency of specialization or differentiation that won out. No matter how the century began, or what were the dreams of a Comte, Spencer, or Marx, when the 19th century ended, not one but several distinct, competitive social sciences were to be found.

Aiding this process was the development of the colleges and universities. With hindsight it might be said that the cause of universities in the future would have been strengthened, as would the cause of the social sciences, had there come into existence, successfully, a single curriculum, undifferentiated by field, for the study of society. What in fact happened, however, was the opposite.

The growing desire for an elective system, for a substantial number of academic specializations, and for differentiation of academic degrees, contributed strongly to the differentiation of the social sciences. This was first and most strongly to be seen in Germany, where, from about 1815 on, all scholarship and science were based in the universities and where competition for status among the several disciplines was keen. But by the end of the century the same phenomenon of specialization was to be found in the United States (where admiration for the German system was very great in academic circles) and, in somewhat less degree, in France and England.

Admittedly, the differentiation of the social sciences in the 19th century was but one aspect of a larger process that was to be seen as vividly in the physical sciences and the humanities. No major field escaped the lure of specialization of investigation, and clearly, a great deal of the sheer bulk of learning that passed from the 19th to the 20th century was the direct consequence of this specialization.

5.2 Social-systems approach

Still another major tendency in all of the social sciences since World War II has been the interest in "social systems." The behaviour of individuals and groups is seen as falling into multiple interdependencies, and these interdependencies are considered sufficiently unified to warrant use of the word "system." Although there are clear uses of biological models and concepts in social-systems work, it may be fair to say that the greatest single impetus to development of this area was widening interest after World War II in cybernetics--the study of human control functions and of the electrical and mechanical systems that could be devised to replace or reinforce them. Concepts drawn from mechanical and electrical engineering have been rather widespread in the study of social systems.

In social-systems studies, the actions and reactions of individuals, or even of groups as large as nations, are seen as falling within certain definable, more or less universal patterns of equilibrium and disequilibrium. The interdependence of roles, norms, and functions is regarded as fundamental in all types of group behaviour, large and small. Each social system, as encountered in social-science studies, is a kind of "ideal type," not identical to any specific "real" condition but sufficiently universal in terms of its central elements to permit useful generalization.

5.3 Social psychology

Social psychology as a distinct discipline also originated in the 19th century, although its outlines were perhaps somewhat less clear than was true of the other social sciences. The close relation of the human mind to the social order, its dependence upon education and other forms of socialization, was well known in the 18th century.

In the 19th century, however, an ever more systematic discipline came into being to uncover the social and cultural roots of human psychology and also the several types of "collective mind" that analysis of different cultures and societies in the world might reveal.

In Germany, Moritz Lazarus and Wilhelm Wundt sought to fuse the study of psychological phenomena with analyses of whole cultures. Folk psychology, as it was called, did not, however, last very long in scientific esteem.

Much more esteemed, and closer to 20th-century conceptions of social psychology, were the works of such men as Gabriel Tarde, Gustave Le Bon, Lucien Lévy-Bruhl, and Émile Durkheim in France and Georg Simmel in Germany (all of whom also wrote in the early 20th century).

Here, in concrete, often highly empirical studies of small groups, associations, crowds, and other aggregates (rather than in the main line of psychology during the century, which tended to be sheer philosophy at one extreme and a variant of physiology at the other) are to be found the real beginnings of social psychology.

Although the point of departure in each of the studies was the nature of association, they dealt, in one degree or other, with the internal processes of psychosocial interaction, the operation of attitudes and judgments, and the social basis of personality and thought--in short, with those phenomena that would, in the 20th century, be the substance of social psychology as a formal discipline.

5.4 Twenty-first century social science

What is seen in the 21st century is not only an intensification and spread of earlier tendencies in the social sciences but also the development of many new tendencies that, in the aggregate, make the

19th and 20th century seem by comparison one of quiet unity and simplicity in the social sciences.

In the 21st century, the processes first generated by the democratic and industrial revolutions have gone on virtually unchecked in Western society, penetrating more and more spheres of once traditional morality and culture, leaving their impress on more and more nations, regions, and localities.

Equally important, perhaps in the long run far more so, is the spread of these revolutionary processes to the non-Western areas of the world. The impact of industrialism, technology, secularism, and individualism upon peoples long accustomed to the ancient unities of tribe, local community, agriculture, and religion was first to be seen in the context of colonialism, an outgrowth of nationalism and capitalism in the West.

The relations of the West to non-Western parts of the world, the whole phenomenon of the "new nations," are vital aspects of the social sciences.

So too are certain other consequences, or lineal episodes, of the two revolutions. The 21st century is the century of nationalism, mass democracy, and large-scale industrialism beyond reach of any 19th-20th century imagination so far as magnitude is concerned.

It is the century of mass warfare, with toll in lives and property greater perhaps than the sum total of all preceding wars in history. It is the century too of totalitarianism: Communism in new countries, neo-Fascism, and neo-Nazism; and of techniques of terrorism that, if not novel, are to be seen on a scale and with an intensity of scientific application that could scarcely have been predicted by those who considered science and technology as unqualifiedly humane in possibility.

It is a century of the continuous affluence in the West, without precedent for the masses of people, to be seen in a constantly rising standard of living and a constantly rising level of expectations.

The last is important. A great deal of the turbulence in the 21st century--political, economic, and social--is the result of desires and aspirations that have been constantly escalating and that have been passing from the white people in the West to ethnic and racial minorities among them and, then, to whole continents elsewhere.

Of all manifestations of revolution, the revolution of rising expectations is perhaps the most powerful in its consequences. For, once this revolution gets under way, each fresh victory in the struggle for rights, freedom, and security tends to magnify the importance of what has not been won.

5.5 Amelioration of other problems

Once it was thought that, by solving the fundamental problems of production and large-scale organization, man could ameliorate other problems, those of a social, moral, and psychological nature. What in fact occurred, on the testimony of a great deal of the most notable thought and writing, was a heightening of such problems.

It would appear that as man satisfies, relatively at least, the lower order needs of food and shelter, his higher order needs for purpose and meaning in life become ever more imperious.

Thus such philosophers of history as Arnold Toynbee, Pitirim Sorokin, and Oswald Spengler have dealt with problems of purpose and meaning in history with a degree of learning and intensity of spirit not seen perhaps since St. Augustine wrote his monumental *The City of God* in the early 5th century when signs of the disintegration of Roman civilization were becoming overwhelming in their message to so many of that day.

In the 21st century, though the idea of progress has certainly not disappeared, it has been rivalled by ideas of cyclical change and of degeneration of society. It is hard to miss the currency of ideas in modern times--status, community, purpose, moral integration, on the one hand, and alienation, anomie, disintegration, breakdown on the other--that reveal only too clearly the divided nature of man's spirit, the unease of his mind.

There is to be seen too, especially during later decades of the century, a questioning of the role of reason in human affairs--a questioning that stands in stark contrast with the ascendancy of rationalism in the two or three centuries preceding.

Doctrines and philosophies stressing the inadequacy of reason, the subjective character of human commitment, and the primacy of faith have rivalled--some would say conquered--doctrines and philosophies descended from the Age of Reason.

Existentialism, with its emphasis on the basic loneliness of the individual, on the impossibility of finding truth through intellectual decision, and on the irredeemably personal, subjective character of man's life, has proved to be a very influential philosophy in the writings of the 20th century.

Freedom, far from being the essence of hope and joy, is the source of man's dread of the universe and of his anxiety for himself. Søren Kierkegaard's 19th-century intimations of anguished isolation as the perennial lot of the individual have had rich expression in the philosophy and literature of the 20th century.

It might be thought that such intimations and presentiments as these have little to do with the social sciences. This is true in the direct sense perhaps but not true when one examines the matter in terms of contexts and ambiences.

The "lost individual" has been of as much concern to the social sciences as to philosophy and literature. Ideas of alienation, anomie, identity crisis, and estrangement from norms are rife among the social sciences, particularly, of course, those most directly concerned with the nature of the social bond, such as sociology, social psychology, and political science.

In countless ways, interest in the loss of community, in the search for community, and in the individual's relation to society and morality have had expression in the work of the social sciences. Between the larger interests of a culture and the social sciences there is never a wide gulf--only different ways of defining and approaching these interests.

5.6 Theoretical modes

It is not the case that interest in theory is a casualty of the 20th-century fascination with method and fact. Though there is a great deal less of that grand or comprehensive theory that was a hallmark of 19th-century social philosophy and social science, there are still those persons occasionally to be found today who are engrossed in search for master principles, for general and unified theory that will assimilate all the lesser and more specialized types of theory. But their efforts and results are not regarded as successful by the vast majority of social scientists.

Theory, at its best, today tends to be specific theory--related to one or other of the major divisions of research within each of the social sciences. The theory of the firm in economics, of deviance in sociology, of communication in political science, of attitude formation in social psychology, of divergent development in cultural anthropology are all examples of theory in every proper sense of the word. But each is, clearly, specific.

If there is a single social science in which a more or less unified theory exists, with reference to the whole of the discipline, it is economics. Even here, however, unified, general theory does not have the sovereign sweep it had in the classical tradition of Ricardo and his followers before the true complexities of economic behaviour had become revealed.

5.7 Developmentalism

Developmentalism is another overall influence upon the work of the social sciences, especially within the past three decades. As noted above, an interest in social evolution was one of the major aspects of the social sciences throughout the 19th century in Western Europe. In the early 20th century, however, this interest, in its larger and more visible manifestations, seemed to terminate. There was a widespread reaction against the idea of unilinear sequences of stages, deemed by the 19th-century social evolutionists to be universal for all mankind in all places.

Criticism of social evolution in this broad sense was a marked element of all the social sciences, pre-eminently in anthropology but in the others as well. There were numerous demonstrations of the inadequacy of unilinear descriptions of change when it came to accounting for what actually happened, so far as records and other evidences suggested, in the different areas and cultures of the world.

Beginning in the late 1940s and the 1950s, however, there was a resurgence of developmental ideas in all the social sciences-- particularly with respect to studies of the new nations and cultures that were coming into existence in considerable numbers. Studies of economic growth and of political and social development have become more and more numerous.

Although it would be erroneous to see these developmental studies as simple repetitions of those of the 19th-century social evolutionists, there are, nevertheless, common elements of thought, including the idea of stages of growth and of change conceived as continuous and cumulative and even as moving toward some more or less common end. At their best, these studies of growth and development in the new nations, by their counter-posing of traditional and modern ways, tell a good deal about specific mechanisms of change, the result of the impact of the West upon outlying parts of the world.

But as more and more social scientists have recently become aware, efforts to place these concrete mechanisms of change into larger, more systematic models of development all too commonly succumb to the same faults of unilinearity and specious universalism that early-20th-century critics found in 19th-century social evolution.

5.8 Marxist influences

The influence of Marxism in the 20th century must not be missed. Currently the works of Lenin have outstripped the Bible in distribution in the world. For hundreds of millions of persons today the ideas of Marx, as communicated by Lenin, have profound moral, even religious, significance.

But even in those parts of the world, the West foremost, where Communism has exerted little direct political impact, Marxism remains a potent source of ideas. Not a few of the central concepts of social stratification and the location and diffusion of power in the social sciences come straight from Marx's insights.

Far more was this the case in the Communist countries--the former Soviet Union, other eastern European countries, China, and even Asian countries in which no Communist domination exists. In all these countries, Marx's name is virtually sacrosanct. There is not the same degree of differentiation of social sciences in these countries that is found in the West.

As an example, sociology hardly exists as a recognized discipline in these countries, and, by the standards of the West, the other social sciences have little more than a rather rudimentary existence. Economics alone tends to be favoured, and this is, of course, largely Marxian economics--the economics of Marx's *Das Kapital*.

But, though Marxism has had relatively little direct impact on the social sciences as disciplines in the West, it has had enormous influence on states of mind that are closely associated with the social sciences. Especially was this true during the 1930s, the decade of the Great Depression.

Today signs are not lacking of a strong revival of interest in Marx that could well, through sheer numbers of its adherents, affect the nature of the social sciences in the years ahead. Socialism remains for many an evocative symbol and creed. Marx remains a formidable name among intellectuals and is still, without any question, the principal intellectual source of radical movements in politics. Such a position cannot help but influence the contexts of even the most abstract of the social sciences.

What Marx's ideas have suggested above all else in a positive way is the possibility of a society directed not by blind forces of competition and struggle among economic elements but instead by directed planning. This hope, this image, has proved a dominant one in the 20th century even where the influence of Marx and of Socialism has been at best small and indirect.

It is this profound interest in central planning and governance that has given almost historic significance to the ideas of the English economist J.M. Keynes. What is called Keynesianism has as its intellectual base a very complex modification of the classical doctrines of economics--one set forth in Keynes's famous *The General Theory of Employment, Interest and Money*, published in 1935-36.

Of greater influence today, however, than the strictly theoretical content of this general theory is the political impact that Keynesian ideas have had on Western democracies. For out of these ideas came the clear policy of governments dealing directly with the business cycle, of pumping money and credit into an economic system when the cycle threatens to turn downward, and of then lessening this infusion when the cycle moves upward.

Above all other names in the West, that of Keynes has become identified with such policy in the democracies and with the general movement of central governments toward ever more active and constant regulation of processes once thought best left to what the classical economists thought of as natural laws.

True, the root ideas of the classical economists are found in modified form even today in the works of such economists as the American Milton Friedman. But it would not be unfair to say that Keynes's name has become associated with democratic economic planning and direction in much the way that Marx's name is associated with Communist economic policies.

5.9 Heritage of the Enlightenment

There is also the fact that, especially in the 18th century, reform and even revolution were often in the air. The purpose of a great many social philosophers was by no means restricted to philosophic, much less scientific, understanding of man and society. The dead hand of the Middle Ages seemed to many vigorous minds in western Europe the principal force to be combated, through critical reason, enlightenment, and, where necessary, major reform or revolution.

One may properly account a great deal of this new spirit to the rise of humanitarianism in modern Europe and in other parts of the world and to the spread of literacy, the rise in the standard of living, and the recognition that poverty and oppression need not be the fate of the masses.

The fact remains, however, that social reform and social science have different organizing principles, and the very fact that for a long time, down indeed through a good part of the 19th century, social reform and social science were regarded as pretty much the same thing could not have helped but retard the development of the latter.

Nevertheless, it would be wrong to discount the significant contributions to the social sciences that were made during the 17th and 18th centuries. The first and greatest of these was the spreading ideal of a science of society, an ideal fully as widespread by the 18th century as the ideal of a physical science. Second was the rising awareness of the multiplicity and variety of human experience in the world.

5.10 Ethnocentrism and parochialism

Ethnocentrism and parochialism, as states of mind, were more and more difficult for educated people to maintain given the immense amount of information about--or, more important, interest in--non-Western peoples, the results of trade and exploration. Third was the spreading sense of the social or cultural character of human behaviour in society--that is, its purely historical or conventional, rather than biological, basis. A science of society, in short, was no mere appendage of biology but was instead a distinct discipline, or set of disciplines, with its own distinctive subject matter.

To these may be added two other very important contributions of the 17th and 18th centuries, each of great theoretical importance. The first was the idea of structure. First seen in the writings of such philosophers as Hobbes, Locke, and Rousseau with reference to the political structure of the state, it had spread by the mid-18th century to highlight the economic writings of the Physiocrats and Adam Smith.

The idea of structure can also be seen in certain works relating to man's psychology and, at opposite reach, to the whole of civil society. The ideas of structure that were borrowed from both the physical and biological sciences were fundamental to the conceptions of political, economic, and social structure that took shape in the 17th and 18th centuries. And these conceptions of structure have in many instances, subject only to minor changes, come down to 20th-century social science.

The second major theoretical idea was that of developmental change. Its ultimate roots in Western thought, like those indeed of the whole idea of structure, go back to the Greeks, if not earlier. But it is in the 18th century, above all others, that the philosophy of Developmentalism took shape, forming a preview, so to speak, of the social evolutionism of the next century.

What was said by such writers as Condorcet, Rousseau, and Adam Smith was that the present is an outgrowth of the past, the result of a long line of development in time, and, furthermore, a line of development that has been caused, not by God or fortuitous factors, but by conditions and causes immanent in human society. Despite a fairly widespread belief that the idea of social development is a product of prior discovery of biological evolution, the facts are the reverse.

Well before any clear idea of genetic speciation existed in European biology, there was a very clear idea of what might be called social speciation--that is, the emergence of one institution from another in time and of the whole differentiation of function and structure that goes with this emergence.

As has been suggested, these and other seminal ideas were contained for the most part in writings, the primary function of which was attack on the existing order of government and society in western Europe. Another way of putting the matter is to say that they were clear and acknowledged parts of political and social idealism--using that word in its largest sense. Hobbes, Locke, Rousseau, Montesquieu, Adam Smith, and other major philosophers had as vivid and energizing sense of the ideal--ideal state, ideal economy, ideal civil society--as any earlier utopian writer.

These men were, without exception, committed to visions of the good or ideal society. Their interest in the "natural"--that is, natural morality, religion, economy, or education, in contrast to the merely conventional and historically derived--sprang as much from the desire to hold a glass up to a surrounding society that they disliked as from any dispassionate urge simply to find out what man and society are made of.

The fact remains, however, that the ideas that were to prove decisive in the 19th century, so far as the social sciences were concerned, arose during the two centuries preceding.

5.11 Freudian influences

In the general area of personality, mind, and character, the writings of Sigmund Freud have had influence on 20th-century culture and thought scarcely less than Marx's. His basic theories of the role of the unconscious mind, of the lasting effects of infantile sexuality, and of the Oedipus complex have gone beyond the discipline of psychoanalysis and even the larger area of psychiatry to areas of several of the social sciences.

Anthropologists have applied Freudian concepts to their studies of primitive cultures, seeking to assess comparatively the universality of states of the unconscious that Freud and his followers held to lie in the whole human race. Some political scientists have used Freudian ideas to illuminate the nature of authority generally and political power specifically, seeing in totalitarianism, for example, the thrust of a craving for the security that total power can give. Sociology and social psychology have been influenced by Freudian ideas in their studies of social interaction and motivation.

From Freud came the fruitful perspective that sees social behaviour and attitudes as generated not merely by the external situation but also by internal emotional needs springing from childhood--needs for recognition, authority, self-expression. Whatever may be the place directly occupied by Freud's ideas in the social sciences today, his influence upon 20th-century thought and culture generally, not excluding the social sciences, has been hardly less than Marx's.

6. INTELLECT AND PHILOSOPHY

6.1 Powerful tendencies

It is important also to identify three other powerful tendencies of thought that influenced all of the social sciences. The first is a positivism that was not merely an appeal to science but almost reverence for science; the second, humanitarianism; the third, the philosophy of evolution.

The Positivist appeal of science was to be seen everywhere. The rise of the ideal of science in the Age of Reason was noted above. The 19th century saw the virtual institutionalization of this ideal--possibly even canonization. The great aim was that of dealing with moral values, institutions, and all social phenomena through the same fundamental methods that could be seen so luminously in such areas as physics and biology.

Prior to the 19th century, no very clear distinction had been made between philosophy and science, and the term philosophy was even preferred by those working directly with physical materials, seeking laws and principles in the fashion of a Newton or Harvey--that is, by persons whom one would now call scientists.

In the 19th century, in contrast, the distinction between philosophy and science became an overwhelming one. Virtually every area of man's thought and behaviour was thought by a rising number of persons to be amenable to scientific investigation in precisely the same degree that physical data were.

6.2 Scientific treatment

More than anyone else, it was Comte who heralded the idea of the scientific treatment of social behaviour. His *Cours de philosophie positive*, published in six volumes between 1830 and 1842, sought to demonstrate irrefutably not merely the possibility but the inevitability of a science of man, one for which Comte coined the word "sociology" and that would do for man the social being exactly what biology had already done for man the biological animal. But Comte was far from alone. There were many in the century to join in his celebration of science for the study of society.

6.3 Humanitarianism

Humanitarianism, though a very distinguishable current of thought in the century, was closely related to the idea of a science of society. For the ultimate purpose of social science was thought by almost everyone to be the welfare of society, the improvement of its moral and social condition.

Humanitarianism, strictly defined, is the institutionalization of compassion; it is the extension of welfare and succour from the limited areas in which these had historically been found, chiefly family and village, to society at large. One of the most notable and also distinctive aspects of the 19th century was the constantly rising number of persons, almost wholly from the middle class, who worked directly for the betterment of society.

In the many projects and proposals for relief of the destitute, improvement of slums, amelioration of the plight of the insane, the indigent, and imprisoned, and other afflicted minorities could be seen the spirit of humanitarianism at work. All kinds of associations were formed, including temperance associations, groups and societies for the abolition of slavery and of poverty and for the improvement of literacy, among other objectives.

Nothing like the 19th-century spirit of humanitarianism had ever been seen before in Western Europe--not even in France during the Enlightenment, where interest in mankind's salvation tended to be more intellectual than humanitarian in the strict sense. Humanitarianism and social science were reciprocally related in their purposes. All that helped the cause of the one could be seen as helpful to the other.

6.4 Evolution

The third of the intellectual influences is that of evolution. It affected every one of the social sciences, each of which was as much concerned with the development of things as with their structures. An interest in development was to be found in the 18th century, as noted earlier. But this interest was small and specialized compared with 19th-century theories of social evolution.

The impact of Charles Darwin's *Origin of Species*, published in 1859, was of course great and further enhanced the appeal of the evolutionary view of things. But it is very important to recognize that ideas of social evolution had their own origins and contexts. The evolutionary works of such social scientists as Comte, Herbert Spencer, and Marx had been completed, or well begun, before publication of Darwin's work.

The important point, in any event, is that the idea or the philosophy of evolution was in the air throughout the century, as profoundly contributory to the establishment of sociology as a systematic discipline in the 1830s as to such fields as geology, astronomy, and biology. Evolution was as permeative an idea as the Trinity had been in medieval Europe.

6.5 Structuralism and functionalism

Structuralism in the social sciences is closely related to the theory of the social system. Although there is nothing new about the root concepts of structuralism--they may be seen in one form or other throughout Western thought--there is no question but that in the present century this view of behaviour has become a dominant one in many fields.

At bottom it is a reaction against all tendencies to deal with human thought and behaviour atomistically--that is, in terms of simple, discrete units of either thought, perception, or overt behaviour. In psychology, structuralism in its oldest sense simply declares that perception occurs, with learning following, in terms of experiences or sensations in various combinations, in discernible patterns or gestalten.

In sociology, political science, and anthropology, the idea of structure similarly refers to the repetitive patternings that are found in the study of social, economic, political, and cultural existence. The structuralist contends that no element can be examined or explained outside its context or the pattern or structure of which it is a part. Indeed, it is the patterns, not the elements that are the only valid objects of study.

What is called functionalism in the social sciences today is closely related to structuralism, with the term structural-functional a common one, especially in sociology and anthropology. Function refers to the way in which behaviour takes on significance, not as a discrete act but as the dynamic aspect of some structure.

Biological analogies are common in theories of structure and function in the social sciences. Very common is the image of the biological organ, with its close interdependence to other organs (as the heart to the lung) and the interdependence of activities (as circulation to respiration).

7. HISTORY OF SOCIAL SCIENCES

7.1 European Development

In the social sciences, fresh starts were made on new premises. Anthropology dropped its concern with physique and race and turned to "culture" as the proper unit of scientific study. Similarly in sociology, Durkheim, seconded by Tönnies, Weber, Tarde, and Le Bon, concentrated on "the social fact" as an independent and measurable reality equivalent to a physical datum.

Psychology, also long under the exclusive sway of physics and physiology, now established at the hands of William James that the irreducible element of its subject matter was the "stream of consciousness"--not a compound of atomized "ideas" or "impressions" or "mind-stuff" but a live force in which image and feeling, subconscious drive and purposive interest, were not separable except abstractly.

A last domain of research was mythology, to the significance of which James George Frazer's *The Golden Bough* gave massive witness, thereby exerting proportional influence on literature and criticism.

7.2 Criminal law

Criminal law has been strongly influenced in the past century or two by the social sciences, especially criminology, sociology, and psychology. The empirical methods of the social sciences have been introduced into legal research and have done much to improve legislation and the courts' approach to sentencing, as well as the planning methods of law-enforcement agencies.

7.3 Behavioural norms

The fact that the crime rates in many countries have risen faster than the population has brought into question the relevance of the law itself and whether or not laws against crime actually have an influence on an individual's behaviour.

Various large-scale inquiries have been made into the relation between law and civil order: in the United States, the President's Commission on Law Enforcement and Administration of Justice; in Europe, several research studies sponsored by the Council of Europe; in Germany, the hearings of the Criminal Reform Commission of the Bundestag.

One conclusion emerging from these inquiries is that criminal legislation ought to be restricted to acts that pose a serious threat to public order and that can be effectively dealt with by the police, the courts, and various correctional institutions.

The effort to punish all behaviour that is considered immoral or deviant, such as drunkenness, gambling, disorderly conduct, vagrancy, and petty sex offences, simply multiplies the number of crimes without changing the norms of behaviour.

7.4 Behavioural science

Behavioural science can be any of various disciplines dealing with the subject of human actions, usually including the fields of sociology, social and cultural anthropology, psychology, and behavioural aspects of biology, economics, geography, law, psychiatry, and political science.

The term gained currency in the 1950s in the United States; it is often used synonymously with "social sciences," although some writers distinguish between them.

The term behavioural sciences suggest an approach that is more experimental than that connoted by the older term social sciences.

7.5 Science interactionism

Interaction is still another concept that has had wide currency in the social sciences of the 20th century. Social interaction--or, as it is sometimes called, symbolic interaction--refers to the fact that the relationships among two or more groups or human beings are never one-sided, purely physical, or direct.

Always there is reciprocal influence, a mutual sense of "otherness." And always the presence of the "other" has crucial effect in one's definition of not merely what is external but what is internal. One acquires one's individual sense of identity from interactions with others beginning in infancy.

It is the initial sense of the other person--mother, for example--that in time gives the child its sense of self, a sense that requires continuous development through later interactions with others.

From the point of view of interactionist theory, all one's perceptions of and reactions to the external world are mediated or influenced by prior ideas, valuations, and assessments. Always one is engaged in socialization or the modification of one's mind, role, and behaviour through contact with others.

8. HERITAGE AND EFFECTS OF THEOLOGY

8.1 Philosophy and theology

The same impulses that led men in that age to explore the earth, the stellar regions, and the nature of matter led them also to explore the institutions around them: state, economy, religion, morality; above all, the nature of man himself.

It was the fragmentation of medieval philosophy and theory, and, with this, the shattering of the medieval world view that had lain deep in thought until about the 16th century, that was the immediate basis of the rise of the several strands of specialized thought that were to become in time the social sciences.

Medieval theology, especially as it appears in St. Thomas Aquinas' *Summa theologiae*, contained and fashioned syntheses from ideas about man and society--ideas indeed that may be seen to be political, social, economic, anthropological, and geographical in their substance.

But it was partly this close relation between medieval theology and ideas of the social sciences that accounts for the longer time it took these ideas—by comparison with the ideas of the physical sciences--to achieve what one would today call scientific character.

From the time of the great Roger Bacon in the 13th century, there were at least some rudiments of physical science that were largely independent of medieval theology and philosophy.

8.2 History and scientists

Historians of physical science have no difficulty in tracing the continuation of this experimental tradition, primitive and irregular though it was by later standards, throughout the Middle Ages. Side by side with the kinds of experiment made notable by Roger Bacon were impressive changes in technology through the medieval period and then, in striking degree, in the Renaissance.

Efforts to improve agricultural productivity; the rising utilization of gunpowder, with consequent development of guns and the problems that they presented in ballistics; growing trade, leading to increased use of ships and improvements in the arts of navigation, including use of telescopes.

The whole range of such mechanical arts in the Middle Ages and Renaissance as architecture, engineering, optics, and the construction of watches and clocks--all of this put a high premium on a pragmatic and operational understanding of at least the simpler principles of mechanics, physics, astronomy, and, in time, chemistry.

In short, by the time of Copernicus and Galileo in the 16th century, a fairly broad substratum of physical science existed, largely empirical but not without theoretical implications on which the edifice of modern physical science could be built.

8.3 Empirical foundations

It is notable that the empirical foundations of physiology were being established in the studies of the human body being conducted in medieval schools of medicine and, as the career of Leonardo da Vinci so resplendently illustrates, among artists of the Renaissance, whose interest in accuracy and detail of painting and sculpture led to their careful studies of human anatomy.

Very different was the beginning of the social sciences. In the first place, the church, throughout the Middle Ages and even into the Renaissance and Reformation, was much more attentive to what scholars wrote and thought about man's mind and his behaviour in society than it was toward what was being studied and written in the physical sciences.

From the church's point of view, while it might be important to see to it that thought on the physical world corresponded as far as possible to what Scripture said--witnessed, for example, in the famous questioning of Galileo--it was far more important that such correspondence exist in matters affecting the nature of man, his mind, spirit, and soul.

Nearly all the subjects and questions that would form the bases of the social sciences in later centuries were tightly woven into the fabric of medieval scholasticism, and it was not easy for even the boldest minds to break this fabric.

8.4 Historical political science

The effort to establish a value-free, objective political science in the United States in the two decades after World War II has won what is doubtless a permanent place for the scientific study of politics, but it also has bred a critical reaction. In the late 1960s opponents of "scientism" rejected what they felt was the increasing subjection of

42

spontaneity and human values to determinisms in every aspect of life and argued that political science was an example of the pervasiveness of technology and of a search for rationality in a social complex that might be irrational and out of control.

Although political science had developed skilful and sensitive techniques for the quantification of data termed political, there is no orthodoxy on the scope of political science nor on the delimitation of separate areas of research. Quite different outcomes emerge from the basic assumptions as to the focus of the discipline, whether it be power, government, system, process, decision making, or policy formulation.

The failure of the discipline to settle the question of identity has made for a creative and inventive exploration of many avenues of research, but the achievement of a unified general theory of political behaviour on which there is common consent still lies ahead.

Even outside the United States, non-normative political science is not extensive, although it is not unknown. England has made many creative contributions to political theory and law throughout its history, as have other European countries, but it also has produced substantial works that can be classified as positive (*i.e.*, non-normative) political science.

Among these are the studies of R.T. McKenzie and D.E. Butler in the field of political parties, voter behaviour, and pressure groups, S.E. Finer on interest groups, and U.W. Kitzinger on German elections. Notable work has been done in France in the field of political parties by Maurice Duverger and François Goguel. Work also has been done on the political socialization of children in French schools by Charles Roig and François Billon-Grand.

In Denmark beginnings were made in the systematic study of political science in 1959 with the founding of the Institute of Governmental Studies at the University of Århus.

In Finland the first extensive studies on voting behaviour appeared in 1956.

In Japan there was a flowering of social sciences after World War II, but political science at first did not grow at the same pace as other social sciences because of lack of agreement about both subject matter and method, a difficulty felt from the beginning by the man recognized to be the founder of Japanese academic political science, Onozuka Kiheiji, who published *Principles of Political Science* in 1903.

With the opening of the behaviour of public officials and institutions to scientific scrutiny, however, there has been much political inquiry that would qualify as political science, including, for example, systems analysis and works on political culture, political development, and process and behaviour.

Although in the past the objective study of political subjects by researchers in Communist regimes has been difficult, if not impossible, a somewhat more permissive policy in some countries has led to what may be the beginnings of scholarly political science. The most advanced political science is to be found in Poland and Yugoslavia, and Romania, the Czech Republic, and Slovakia have come to recognize political science as a discipline.

The former Soviet Union did not sanction political science, but scholars did conduct empirical research, which was endorsed in 1962 by the U.S.S.R. Academy of Sciences under the term "concrete sociological investigations." The greatest movement has been in the conduct of public-opinion polls using advanced Western techniques.

Interest in the development of political science was evidenced in the publication in 1969 of *Politicheskaya nauka v SShA: Kritika burzhuaznykh Kontseptsy vlasti* ("Political Science in the U.S.A.: A Critique of Bourgeois Conceptions of Power"), by V.G. Kalensky. Although there was no officially sanctioned political science, there was a Soviet Association of Political Sciences, which sent delegates to the meeting of the International Political Science Association. Despite its title, the Soviet Association of Political Sciences was most heavily oriented toward the state and the law, and its members were critical of what they regarded as the anti-Marxist bias of bourgeois political science.

One of its members, however, F.M. Burlatsky, published a major article in *Pravda* in 1965 calling for the establishment of a genuine political science in which the findings would emerge from the data.

In Yugoslavia a political-science association was established in 1951, and in 1962 a faculty of the political sciences was established at the University of Zagreb. In Czechoslovakia a political-science association was formed in 1965 and became a member of the International Political Science Association; and in 1968 a political-science association was formed in Romania. Political science in Yugoslav universities has tended to centre on traditional divisions of the discipline, such as political theory, comparative government, and international relations.

In Poland political science has centred on the study of political behaviour, on community power structures, on voter behaviour, and on public opinion. Techniques of considerable sophistication have been employed.

Political science is one of the means by which people seek to understand the human condition and man's fate. Or, as Aristotle believed, politics is the most important of human activities, and the sovereign science. For 24 centuries, at least, the greatest intellects and scholars have striven to state the universal elements of just order in human affairs.

None has succeeded in this, so far, hopeless ambition, although most have contributed some special insight and added to the common wisdom. The effort to achieve magisterial comprehension will doubtless continue; and the search will change direction as experience requires, with the aid that new perceptions, concepts, and methods will provide.

Progress toward establishing general laws, however, may never be as steady or as swift in political science as it has been in laboratory sciences like physics; for, as Albert Einstein once said, politics is more difficult than physics.

8.5 Overpopulation

Overpopulation means an excess of people in relation to the resources available to sustain them. The UN's forecast of population growth suggests that between 1990 and 2025 the world's population will increase from 5.3 billion to 8.5 billion. Almost all of this increase will occur in the developing countries of Asia, Africa, and Latin America. By the late 1980s, 67 nations with 85 per cent of the developing world's population officially considered their growth rates too high.

The UN Population Fund now argues that environmental degradation is the gravest immediate threat posed by over-population, rather than shortages of food, fuel, and minerals as previously thought. Overpopulation (together with excessive consumption by the developed world) is already contributing to desertification, loss of agricultural productivity through overuse of land, the destruction of forests and, through the increased burning of fossil fuels, the greenhouse effect.

Already many poor countries, especially in sub-Saharan Africa, are losing their ability to feed, shelter, and educate even their present populations, yet these are the very countries where population growth is expected to be highest. The UN Population Fund believes that only development can stabilize the world's population and calls for sanitation, education, health care, and family planning in order to reduce fertility rates.

However, the youthful age structure of the world's population and the opposition of the Roman Catholic Church to family planning, especially in South America, mean that overpopulation is one of the severest challenges facing the planet.

8.6 Social sciences in the nineteenth century

The fundamental ideas, themes, and problems of the social sciences in the 19th century are best understood as responses to the problem of order that was created in men's minds by the weakening of the old order, or European society, under the twin blows of the French Revolution and the Industrial Revolution.

The break-up of the old order--an order that had rested on kinship, land, social class, religion, local community, and monarchy--set free, as it were, the complex elements of status, authority, and wealth that had been for so long consolidated. In the same way that the history of 19th-century politics, industry, and trade is basically about the practical efforts of human beings to reconsolidate these elements, so the history of 19th-century social thought is about theoretical efforts to reconsolidate them--that is, to give them new contexts of meaning.

In terms of the immediacy and sheer massiveness of impact on human thought and values, it would be difficult to find revolutions of comparable magnitude in human history. The political, social, and cultural changes that began in France and England at the very end of the 18th century spread almost immediately through Europe and the Americas in the 19th century and then on to Asia, Africa, and Oceania in the 20th.

The effects of the two revolutions, the one overwhelmingly democratic in thrust, the other industrial-capitalist, have been to undermine, shake, or topple institutions that had endured for centuries, even millennia, and with them systems of authority, status, belief, and community.

It is easy today to deprecate the suddenness, the cataclysmic nature, the overall revolutionary effect of these two changes and to seek to subordinate results to longer, deeper tendencies of more gradual change in Western Europe.

But as many recent historians have pointed out, there was to be seen, and seen by a great many sensitive minds of that day, a dramatic and convulsive quality to the changes that cannot properly be subsumed to the slower processes of continuous evolutionary change.

What is crucial, in any event, from the point of view of the history of the social thought of the period, is how the changes were actually envisaged at the time. By a large number of social philosophers and social scientists, in all spheres, those changes were regarded as nothing less than of earthquake intensity.

The coining or redefining of words is an excellent indication of men's perceptions of change in a given historical period. A large number of words taken for granted today came into being in the period marked by the final decade or two of the 18th century and the first quarter of the 19th. Among these are: industry, industrialist, democracy, class, middle class, ideology, intellectual, rationalism, humanitarian, atomistic, masses, commercialism, proletariat, collectivism, equalitarian, liberal, conservative, scientist, utilitarian, bureaucracy, capitalism, and crisis.

Some of these words were invented; others reflect new and very different meanings given to old ones. All alike bear witness to the transformed character of the European social landscape as this landscape loomed up to the leading minds of the age. And all these words bear witness too to the emergence of new social philosophies and, most pertinent to the subject of this article, the social sciences as they are known today.

8.7 Cultural anthropology

In the 19th century, anthropology also attained clear identity as a discipline. Strictly defined as "the science of man," it could be seen as superseding other specialized disciplines such as economics and political science.

In practice and from the beginning, however, anthropology concerned itself overwhelmingly with primitive man. On the one hand was physical anthropology, concerned chiefly with the evolution of man as a biological species, with the successive forms and protoforms of the species, and with genetic systems such as stocks and races in the world.

On the other hand was social and cultural anthropology: here the interest was in the full range of man's institutions but confined to those found in fact among existing preliterate or "primitive" peoples in

Africa, Oceania, Asia, and the Americas. Above all other concepts, "culture" was the central element of this great area of anthropology, or ethnology, as it was often called to distinguish it from physical anthropology.

Culture, as a concept, called attention to the non-biological, non-racial, non-instinctual basis of the greater part of what one calls civilization: its values, techniques, ideas in all spheres. Culture, as defined in Tylor's landmark work of 1871, *Primitive Culture*, is the part of man's behaviour that is learned. From cultural anthropology more than from any other single social science has come the emphasis on the cultural foundations of man's behaviour and thought in society.

Scarcely less than political science or economics, cultural anthropology shared in the themes of the two revolutions and their impact on the world. If the data that cultural anthropologists actually worked with were generally in the remote areas of the world, it was the effects of the two revolutions that, in a sense, kept opening up these parts of the world to more and more systematic inquiry. And, as was true of the other social sciences, the cultural anthropologists were immersed in problems of economics, polity, social class, and community, albeit among preliterate rather than "modern" peoples.

Overwhelmingly, without major exception indeed, the science of cultural anthropology was evolutionary in thrust in the 19th century. Edward B. Tylor and Sir John Lubbock in England, Lewis Henry Morgan in the United States, Adolf Bastian and Theodor Waitz in Germany, and all others in the main line of the study of primitive culture saw existing native societies in the world as prototypes of their own "primitive ancestors," fossilized remains, so to speak, of stages of development that western Europe had once gone through.

Despite the vast array of data compiled on non-Western cultures, the same basic European-centred objectives are to be found among cultural anthropologists as among other social scientists in the century. Almost universally, then, the modern West was regarded as the latest point in a line of progress that was single and unilinear and on which all other peoples in the world could be fitted as illustrations, as it were, of Western man's own past.

9. POLITICAL SCIENCE

9.1 Politics rivalling economics

Rivalling economics as a discipline during the century was political science. The line of systematic interest in the state that had begun in modern Europe with Machiavelli, Hobbes, Locke, and Rousseau, among others, widened and lengthened in the 19th century, the consequence of the two revolutions.

If the Industrial Revolution seemed to supply all the problems frustrating the existence of a stable and humane society, the political-democratic revolution could be seen as containing many of the answers to these problems. It was the democratic revolution, especially in France, that created the vision of a political government responsible for all aspects of human society and, most important, possessed the power to wield this responsibility.

This power, known as sovereignty, could be seen as holding the same relation to political science in the 19th century that capital held to economics. To a very large number of political scientists, the aim of the discipline was essentially that of analyzing the varied properties of sovereignty.

There was a strong tendency on the part of such political scientists as Bentham, Austin, and Mill in England and Francis Lieber and Woodrow Wilson in the United States to see the state and its claimed sovereignty over human lives in much the same terms in which classical economists saw capitalism.

9.2 Political scientists

Among political scientists there was the same historical-evolutionary dissent from this view, however, that existed in economics. Such writers as Sir Henry Maine in England, Numa Fustel de Coulanges in France, and Otto von Gierke in Germany declared that state and sovereignty were not timeless and universal nor the results of some "social contract" envisaged by such philosophers as Locke and Rousseau but, rather, structures formed slowly through developmental or historical processes.

Hence the strong interest, especially in the late 19th century, in the origins of political institutions in kinship, village, and caste, and in the successive stages of development that have characterized these institutions. In political science, as in economics, in short, the classical analytical approach was strongly rivalled by the evolutionary.

Both approaches go back to the 18th century in their fundamental elements, but what is seen in the 19th century is the greater systematization and the much wider range of data employed.

9.3 Early trends of political science

The origins of contemporary political science are to be found in the enthusiasm for the creation of social science that was widespread in the 19th century, an enthusiasm stimulated by the rapid growth of the natural sciences. It might be said that one starting point for the development of modern political science is the work of the Comte Henri de Saint-Simon, a notable Utopian Socialist, who in 1813 suggested that morals and politics could become "positive" sciences; that is, disciplines whose authority to command belief would rest not upon subjective preconceptions but upon objective evidence.

With him worked the mathematician and philosopher Auguste Comte, the two collaborating in the publication in 1822 of the Plan of the Scientific Operations Necessary for the Reorganization of Society, which argued, among much else, that politics would become social physics and that the purpose of social physics was to discover unchanging laws of progress.

9.4 Emerging law

Out of this collaboration emerged the law of the three stages through which knowledge had to pass--the theological, the metaphysical, and the positive--which Comte was to establish as the theme of the science of social physics, a study he came to name sociology.

An intellectual connection between political science and sociology was thus early established in schemes of political and social regeneration and reform, although political science was thought to be limited to only one form of association in society, namely, the state. Comte thought that the principal methods for the study of social phenomena were observation, experiment, and abstraction.

Although one might have thought that politics could not be an experimental science, Comte was of the view that political experimentation did take place whenever there was a change in the life of the state, intended or not. It must be said, however, that even on this account there is no close similarity to experimentation in chemistry and physics, in which all the variables can be controlled.

9.5 Methods of inquiry

In the search for more objective methods of inquiry into political and other social phenomena in the 19th century, contributions to the explanations of the state were supplied by several new intellectual disciplines. Because political science deals with some aspects of human behaviour, for example, it is closely allied to other social sciences that also deal with human behaviour.

Long before the development of scientific inquiries in the 19th century, numerous theories of the state had drawn inspiration from the human being as model, as in the *Policraticus* of John of Salisbury (1159), in which the physiology of the body and that of the state are compared; or in the Republic of Plato, in which the elements of the human personality prefigure the class structure of the state; and in Rousseau's *Contrat Social*, in which the political order is animated by a general will (will being a human attribute).

The positivism of the 19th century, however, brought new approaches to the study of the state, although the older ones continued to coexist with them. Among those following Comte was the Polish-born sociologist Ludwig Gumplowicz, who built a sociology on Comtean foundations but who owed much also to Darwin, to the social Darwinist Herbert Spencer, and to contemporary anthropology.

In Gumplowicz' view, the earliest forms of group life were small hordes bound by consanguinity, which developed into matriarchies and patriarchies. He supposed the existence of a social-evolutionary process characterized by conflicts between autonomous groups and by conflicts of interest within those groups. The product of this process was the state, founded on force and maintained by power.

Gumplowicz and several other 19th-century political sociologists anticipated 20th-century concerns in political science with the significance of groups, the nature of interests, the role of parties as interest groups, and the social context within which political events occur.

Still another 19th-century writer with some precedental connection to the political science of the 20th was the Italian Vilfredo Pareto. Although he lived and wrote in both the 19th and 20th centuries, he may be counted in the earlier period because of his advocacy of the "logico-experimental" approach to sociology, which involved observation and logical inference.

Pareto had no direct influence on the development of political science, but in two respects his sociology had implications for the developing discipline. First, his was a psychological sociology, and much of his concern was with the influence of beliefs, attitudes, opinions, and sentiments in shaping social life. This anticipates the 20th-century approach of many political scientists who regard psychology as the most important adjunct of the scientific study of politics.

10. SOCIOLOGY

10.1 Society as a system

Social scientists thought of society as a system always tending toward equilibrium, and the conception of politics as a system was to mark much of academic political science after World War II.

In the context of important 19th-century sociological theories is the work of a Swedish political scientist, Rudolf Kjellen, whose systematic treatment of the state as a fusion of organic and intellectual moral elements in an ambience of geographical determinism led to a theory of politics that he termed geopolitics.

Sociology came into being in precisely these terms, and during much of the century it was not easy to distinguish between a great deal of so-called sociology and social or cultural anthropology. Even if almost no sociologists in the century made empirical studies of primitive peoples, as did the anthropologists, their interest in the origin, development, and probable future of mankind was not less great than what could be found in the writings of the anthropologists.

It was Auguste Comte who coined the word sociology, and he used it to refer to what he imagined would be a single, all-encompassing, science of society that would take its place at the top of the hierarchy of sciences--a hierarchy that Comte saw as including astronomy (the oldest of the sciences historically) at the bottom and with physics, chemistry, and biology rising in that order to sociology, the latest and grandest of the sciences.

There was no thought in Comte's mind--nor was there in the mind of Herbert Spencer, whose general view of sociology was very much like Comte's--of there being other, competing social sciences. Sociology would be to the whole of the social world what each of the other great sciences was to its appropriate sphere of reality.

10.2 Civilization as a whole

Both Comte and Spencer believed that civilization as a whole was the proper subject of sociology. Their works were concerned, for the most part, with describing the origins and development of civilization and also of each of its major institutions. Both declared sociology's main divisions to be "statics" and "dynamics," the former concerned with processes of order in society, the latter with processes of evolutionary change in society.

Both men also saw all existing societies in the world as reflective of the successive stages through which Western society had advanced in time over a period of tens of thousands of years.

Not all sociologists in the 19th century conceived their discipline in this light, however. Side by side with the "grand" view represented by Comte and Spencer were those in the century who were primarily interested in the social problems that they saw around them-- consequences, as they interpreted them, of the two revolutions, the industrial and democratic.

Thus in France just after mid-century, Frédéric Le Play published a monumental study of the social aspects of the working classes in Europe, *Les Ouvriers européens*, which compared families and communities in all parts of Europe and even other parts of the world. Alexis de Tocqueville, especially in the second volume of his *Democracy in America* (1835), provided an account of the customs, social structures, and institutions in America, dealing with these--and also with the social and psychological problems of Americans in that day-- as aspects of the impact of the democratic and industrial revolutions upon traditional society.

At the very end of the 19th century, in both France and Germany, there appeared some of the works in sociology that were to prove most lasting in their effects upon 20th-century sociology. Ferdinand Tönnies, in his *Gemeinschaft und Gesellschaft* (1887; translated as *Community and Society*), sought to explain all major social problems in the West as the consequence of the West's historical transition from the communal, status-based, concentric society of the Middle Ages to the more individualistic, impersonal, and large-scale society of the democratic-industrial period.

In general terms, allowing for individual variations of theme, these were the views of Max Weber, Georg Simmel, and Émile Durkheim (all of whom also wrote in the late 19th and early 20th century). These were the men who, starting from the problems of Western society that could be traced to the effects of the two revolutions, did the most to establish the discipline of sociology as it is found for the most part in the 20th century.

10. 3 Effects of the classics and of Cartesianism

Then, when the hold of scholasticism did begin to wane, two fresh influences, equally powerful, came on the scene to prevent anything comparable to the pragmatic and empirical foundations of the physical sciences from forming in the study of man and society. The first was the immense appeal of the Greek classics during the Renaissance, especially those of the philosophers Plato and Aristotle. A great deal of social thought during the Renaissance was little more than gloss or commentary on the Greek classics. One sees this throughout the 15th and 16th centuries.

Second, in the 17th century appeared the powerful influence of the philosopher René Descartes. Cartesianism, as his philosophy was called, declared that the proper approach to understanding of the world, including man and society, was through a few simple, fundamental ideas of reality and, then, rigorous, almost geometrical deduction of more complex ideas and eventually of large, encompassing theories, from these simple ideas, all of which, Descartes insisted, were the stock of common sense--the mind that is common to all human beings at birth.

It would be hard to exaggerate the impact of Cartesianism on social and political and moral thought during the century and a half following publication of his *Discourse on Method* and his *Meditations*. Through the Age of Reason and down through the Enlightenment in the later 18th century, the spell of Cartesianism was cast on nearly all those who were concerned with the problems of the nature of man and society.

Both of these great influences, reverence for the classics and fascination with the geometrical-deductive procedures advocated by Descartes must be seen from today's vantage point as among the major influences retarding the development of a science of society comparable to the science of the physical world. It is not as though data were not available in the 17th and 18th centuries.

The emergence of the national state carried with it ever growing bureaucracies concerned with gathering information, chiefly for taxation, census, and trade purposes, which might have been employed in much the same way that physical scientists employed their data.

The voluminous and widely published accounts of the great voyages that had begun in the 15th century, the records of soldiers, explorers, and missionaries who perforce had been brought into often long and close contact with primitive and other non-Western peoples, provided still another great reservoir of data, all of which might have been utilized in scientific ways as such data were to be utilized a century or two later in the social sciences.

Such, however, was the continuing spell cast by the texts of the classics and by the strictly rationalistic, overwhelmingly deductive procedures of the Cartesians that, down until the beginning of the 19th century, these and other empirical materials were used, if at all, solely for illustrative purposes in the writings of the social philosophers.

11. ECONOMICS

11.1 Single and separate science

It was economics that first attained the status of a single and separate science, in ideal at least, among the social sciences. That autonomy and self-regulation that the Physiocrats and Adam Smith had found, or thought they had found, in the processes of wealth, in the operation of prices, rents, interest, and wages during the 18th century became the basis of a separate and distinctive economics--or, as it was often called, "political economy"--in the 19th.

11.2 Laissez-faire

Hence the emphasis upon what came to be widely called laissez-faire. If, as it was argued, the processes of wealth operate naturally in terms of their own built-in mechanisms, then not only should these be studied separately but they should, in any wise polity, be left alone by government and society.

11.3 Classical in economics

This was, in general, the overriding emphasis of such thinkers as David Ricardo, John Stuart Mill, and Nassau William Senior in England, of Frédéric Bastiat and Jean-Baptiste Say in France, and, somewhat later, the Austrian school of Carl Menger. This emphasis is today called "classical" in economics, and it is even now, though with substantial modifications, a strong position in the field.

11.4 Divergence

There were almost from the beginning, however, economists who diverged sharply from this laissez-faire, classical view. In Germany especially there were the so-called historical economists. They proceeded less from the discipline of historiography than from the presuppositions of social evolution, referred to above.

Such men as Wilhelm Roscher and Karl Knies in Germany tended to dismiss the assumptions of timelessness and universality regarding economic behaviour that were almost axiomatic among the followers of Adam Smith, and they strongly insisted upon the developmental character of capitalism, evolving in a long series of stages from other types of economy.

11.5 Socialists economists

Also prominent throughout the century were those who came to be called the Socialists. They too repudiated any notion of timelessness and universality in capitalism and its elements of private property, competition, and profit. Not only was this system but a passing stage of economic developments; it could be--and, as Marx was to emphasize, would be--shortly supplanted by a more humane and also realistic economic system based upon cooperation, the people's ownership of the means of production, and planning that would eradicate the vices of competition and conflict.

12. NEW IDEOLOGIES

12.1 Conservative, liberal, or radical

One other point must be emphasized about these themes. They became, almost immediately in the 19th century, the bases of new ideologies. How men reacted to the currents of democracy and industrialism stamped them conservative, liberal, or radical. On the whole, with rarest exceptions, liberals welcomed the two revolutions, seeing in their forces opportunity for freedom and welfare never before known to mankind.

The liberal view of society was overwhelmingly democratic, capitalist, industrial, and, of course, individualistic. The case is somewhat different with conservatism and radicalism in the century.

Conservatives, beginning with Edmund Burke, continuing through Hegel and Matthew Arnold down to such minds as John Ruskin later in the century, disliked both democracy and industrialism, preferring the kind of tradition, authority, and civility that had been, in their minds, displaced by the two revolutions.

Theirs was a retrospective view, but it was a nonetheless influential one, affecting a number of the central social scientists of the century, among them Auguste Comte and Tocqueville and later Max Weber and Émile Durkheim.

The radicals accepted democracy but only in terms of its extension to all areas of society and its eventual annihilation of any form of authority that did not spring directly from the people as a whole. And although the radicals, for the most part, accepted the phenomenon of industrialism, especially technology, they were uniformly antagonistic to capitalism.

These ideological consequences of the two revolutions proved extremely important to the social sciences, for it would be difficult to identify a social scientist in the century--as it would a philosopher or a humanist--who was not, in some degree at least, caught up in ideological currents.

In referring to such minds as Saint-Simon, Comte, Le Play among sociologists, to Ricardo, the Frenchman Jean-Baptiste Say, and Marx among economists, to Jeremy Bentham and John Austin among political scientists, even to anthropologists like the Englishman Edward B. Tylor and the American Lewis Henry Morgan, one has before one men who were engaged not merely in the study of society but also in often strongly partisan ideology. Some were liberals, some conservatives, others radicals. All drew from the currents of ideology that had been generated by the two great revolutions.

12.2 Economics

This social science seeks to analyze and describe the production, distribution, and consumption of wealth.

The major divisions of economics include microeconomics, which deals with the behaviour of individual consumers, companies, traders, and farmers; and macroeconomics, which focuses on aggregates such as the level of income in an economy, the volume of total employment, and the flow of investment.

Another branch, development economics, investigates the history and changes of economic activity and organization over a period of time, as well as their relation to other activities and institutions. Within these three major divisions there are specialized areas of study that attempt to answer questions on a broad spectrum of human economic activity, including public finance, money supply and banking, international trade, labour, industrial organization, and agriculture.

The areas of investigation in economics overlap with other social sciences, particularly political science, but economics is primarily concerned with relations between buyer and seller.

12.3 Environmentalism

This is the theory that emphasizes the importance of environmental factors in the development of culture and society.

The theory of environmental determinism states that the physical milieu of a people, including natural resources, climate, and geography, is the major determining factor in the formation of their culture. Determinism thereby rejects history and tradition, social and economic factors, and other aspects of culture as explanations of social development.

Environmental possibilism, an opposing doctrine, suggests that habitat acts only to create possibilities from which people may choose.

Contemporary environmentalists recognize that physical surroundings are only part of a total environment that includes social and economic factors, cultural tradition, and reciprocal influences between societies and their environment.

12.4 Human ecology

Man's collective interaction with his environment is influenced by the work of biologists on the interaction of organisms within their environments; social scientists undertook to study human groups in a similar way.

Thus, ecology in the social sciences is the study of the ways in which the social structure adapts to the quality of natural resources and to the existence of other human groups. When this study is limited to the development and variation of cultural properties, it is called cultural ecology.

Human ecology views the biological, environmental, demographic, and technical conditions of the life of any people as an interrelated series of determinants of form and function in human cultures and social systems.

It recognizes that group behaviour is dependent upon resources and associated skills and upon a body of emotionally charged beliefs; these together give rise to a system of social structures.

12.5 Sociological jurisprudence

The historical jurisprudence of the earlier part of the 19th century became subject to the influence of the developing social sciences, which attempted to explain law in its social context. The result was the emergence of a sociological school of jurisprudence.

The early decades of sociological jurisprudence combined 19th-century faith in progress, social evolution, rationalism, humanitarianism, and political pluralism with a sanguine belief that the Newtonian model of natural science would also hold for the social sciences.

It was affected by questions of whether the social sciences are truly sciences, what their mutual boundaries are, and whether they can be integrated or somehow transcended by some subject such as sociology or anthropology.

An outstanding figure of the early sociological school was a German, Rudolf von Jhering, who in the 1860s contributed to the intellectual stream a theory of justice predicated on a view of law as a social phenomenon. He saw law as an outcome of the struggle of men to fulfil their purposes and of the force that they marshal behind this.

Another historical jurist, the German Otto von Gierke, stirred a related interest with his emphasis on the importance of the inner life and activities of groups and associations as sources of binding social norms. This opened up jurisprudence to some psychological issues. Gierke's work also contributed to the later American Neorealism through its influence on Oliver Wendell Holmes, Jr., and to the theory of the "living law" of the Austrian jurist Eugen Ehrlich, in the first decade of the 20th century. Ehrlich insisted on the profuse norm-creating activities of the countless associations in which men are involved.

At the beginning of the 20th century a great variety of psychological hypotheses were brought to bear on law. A theory of dynamic psychic drives, for example, was propounded by an American sociologist, Lester F. Ward, who argued that such drives could be utilized in social planning. Freud's exploration of psychic activity on a subconscious level, as well as studies of the non-rational and the irrational in the social process by the Italian and German sociologists Vilfredo Pareto and Max Weber, were also profoundly influential.

12.6 Dominant strands of Renaissance

Knowledge in the contemporary world is conventionally divided between the natural sciences, the social sciences, and the humanities. In the Renaissance, however, fields of learning had not yet become so sharply departmentalized: in fact, each of these divisions arose in the comprehensive and broadly inclusive area of Renaissance philosophy.

For, as the Renaissance mounted its revolt against the reign of religion and therefore reacted against the church, against authority, against Scholasticism, and against Aristotle, there was a sudden blossoming of interest in problems centring on civil society, man, and nature.

These three interests found exact representation in the three dominant strands of Renaissance philosophy:

- political theory,

- humanism, and

- philosophy of nature.

12.7 Democratic and industrial themes

It is illuminating to mention a few of the major themes in social thought in the 19th century that were almost the direct results of the democratic and industrial revolutions. It should be borne in mind that these themes are to be seen in the philosophical and literary writing of the age as well as in social thought.

First, there was the great increase in population. Between 1750 and 1850 the population of Europe went from 140,000,000 to 266,000,000; in the world from 728,000,000 to well over 1,000,000,000. It was an English clergyman-economist, Thomas Malthus, who, in his famous *Essay on Population,* first marked the enormous significance to human welfare of this increase.

With the diminution of historic checks on population growth, chiefly those of high mortality rates--a diminution that was, as Malthus realized, one of the rewards of technical progress--there were no easily foreseeable limits to growth of population.

Such growth, he stressed, could only upset the traditional balance between population, which Malthus described as growing at geometrical rate, and food supply, which he declared could grow only at arithmetical rate. Not all social scientists in the century took the pessimistic view of the matter that Malthus did but few if any were indifferent to the impact of explosive increase in population on economy, government, and society.

Second, there was the condition of labour. It may be possible to see this condition in the early 19th century as in fact better than the condition of the rural masses at earlier times. But the important point is that to a large number of writers in the 19th century it seemed worse and was defined as worse.

The wrenching of large numbers of people from the older and protective contexts of village, guild, parish, and family, and their massing in the new centres of industry, forming slums, living in common squalor and wretchedness, their wages generally behind cost of living, their families growing larger, their standard of living becoming lower, as it seemed--all of this is a frequent theme in the social thought of the century.

Economics indeed became known as the "dismal science," because economists, from David Ricardo to Karl Marx, could see little likelihood of the condition of labour improving under capitalism.

Third, there was the transformation of property. Not only was more and more property to be seen as industrial--manifest in the factories, business houses, and workshops of the period--but also the very nature of property was changing.

Whereas for most of the history of mankind property had been "hard," visible only in concrete possessions--land and money--now the more intangible kinds of property such as shares of stock, negotiable equities of all kinds, and bonds were assuming ever greater influence in the economy. This led, as was early realized, to the dominance of financial interests, to speculation, and to a general widening of the gulf between the propertied and the masses.

The change in the character of property made easier the concentration of property, the accumulation of immense wealth in the hands of a relative few, and, not least, the possibility of economic domination of politics and culture. It should not be thought that only socialists saw property in this light. From Edmund Burke through Auguste Comte, Frédéric Le Play, and John Stuart Mill down to Karl Marx, Max Weber, and Émile Durkheim, one finds conservatives and liberals looking at the impact of this change in analogous ways.

Fourth, there was urbanization--the sudden increase in the number of towns and cities in Western Europe and the increase in number of persons living in the historic towns and cities.

Whereas in earlier centuries, the city had been regarded almost uniformly as a setting of civilization, culture, and freedom of mind, now one found more and more writers aware of the other side of cities: the atomization of human relationships, broken families, the sense of the mass, of anonymity, alienation, and disrupted values. Sociology particularly among the social sciences turned its attention to the problems of urbanization.

The contrast between the more organic type of community found in rural areas and the more mechanical and individualistic society of the cities is a basic contrast in sociology, one that was given much attention by such pioneers in Europe as the French sociologists Frédéric Le Play and Émile Durkheim; the German sociologists Ferdinand Tönnies, Georg Simmel, and Max Weber; the Belgian statistician Adolphe Quetelet; and, in America, by the sociologists Charles H. Cooley and Robert E. Park.

Fifth, there was technology. With the spread of mechanization, first in the factories, then in agriculture, social thinkers could see possibilities of a rupture of the historic relation between man and nature, between man and man, even between man and God.

To thinkers as politically different as Thomas Carlyle and Karl Marx, technology seemed to lead to dehumanization of the worker and to exercise of a new kind of tyranny over human life. Marx, though, far from despising technology, thought the advent of socialism would counteract all this.

Alexis de Tocqueville declared that technology, and especially technical specialization of work, was more degrading to man's mind and spirit than even political tyranny. It was thus in the 19th century that the opposition to technology on moral, psychological, and aesthetic grounds first made its appearance in Western thought.

Sixth, there was the factory system. The importance of this to 19th-century thought has been intimated above. Suffice it to add that along with urbanization and spreading mechanization, the system of work whereby masses of workers left home and family to work long hours in the factories became a major theme of social thought as well as of social reform.

Seventh, and finally, mention is to be made of the development of political masses--that is, the slow but inexorable widening of franchise and electorate through which ever larger numbers of persons became aware of themselves as voters and participants in the political process.

This too is a major theme in social thought, to be seen most luminously perhaps in Tocqueville's *Democracy in America*, a classic written in the 1830s that took not merely America but democracy everywhere as its subject. Tocqueville saw the rise of the political masses, more especially the immense power that could be wielded by the masses, as the single greatest threat to individual freedom and cultural diversity in the ages ahead.

These, then, are the principal themes in the 19th-century writing that may be seen as direct results of the two great revolutions. As themes, they are to be found not only in the social sciences but, as noted above, in a great deal of the philosophical and literary writing of the century. In their respective ways, the philosophers Hegel, Coleridge, and Emerson were as struck by the consequences of the revolutions as were any social scientists.

So too were such novelists as Balzac and Dickens.

13. METHODOLOGICAL CONSIDERATIONS

13.1 Behavioural persuasion

In American political science since the end of World War II, the behavioural persuasion has been the dominant one. A former president of the American Political Science Association has attributed the rapid development of the behavioural approach to six causes: the inspiration of the Chicago school; the immigration to the United States in the 1930s of large numbers of European scholars (particularly Germans) with backgrounds in European sociology, who stressed the:

- relevance of sociology to politics;

- movement of many political scientists into administrative and political positions during World War II;

- influence of foundation support in the encouragement of research in political behaviour;

- increasing development of the survey method in certain political studies, such as voter behaviour;

- missionary work of the Social Science Research Council under leadership sympathetic to behaviouralism.

Although the term behaviouralism has been freely used in political-science writings, there is in fact confusion as to whether it is a field of study, a method, or an approach.

One American political scientist, Heinz Eulau, in *The Behavioral Persuasion in Politics* (1963), has said that the behavioural persuasion "is concerned with what man does politically and the meanings he attaches to his behaviour," and he has suggested that researchers cannot afford to get tangled up in problems of definition.

Another American, Robert Dahl, has said that it is a mood or even "the scientific outlook."

The term behavioural, then, may be merely a term having distinctiveness, weight, and value for a certain time only, since it seems primarily to signify that phase in the quarter century after World War II during which there was a significant revival of interest in empirical studies in politics, a movement strong enough to establish at least a partnership with the traditional approaches, although some of its advocates have gone so far as to say that their science has made traditional approaches outdated.

13.2 Social, economic and artistic factors

In order to understand the social and economic factors that influence the creation of art and how it is received, it is necessary to begin a sociological analysis of the arts by identifying the various social frameworks within which artistic activities have been conducted and the influences that these frameworks have had on the style and content of the arts, the levels of creative attainment, the mode of living of the artists, and the uses to which their art has been put by society.

This mode of analysis is not concerned, as the histories of the various arts are, with describing how the particular arts have historically evolved and what they have meant to their users. Rather, it is aimed at discerning the basic alternative patterns of organizing artistic activities and the consequences, for society and for the arts, of adopting one or another of them.

Most of the necessary knowledge for recognizing these patterns is still lacking or is ambiguous in its implications. Indeed, there is no generally accepted theoretical basis for encompassing all the arts in relation to all sociological variables in all types of societies, from the simplest to the most complex.

There is, furthermore, hardly any other field in the whole area between the humanities and the social sciences as inviting to partisan sensibilities as the relationship between art and society. Any general statements about relationships between art and society must therefore be treated cautiously, not as established knowledge but as tentative hypotheses.

13.3 Humanities' modern problems

Contemporary conceptions of the humanities resemble earlier conceptions in that they propose a complete educational program based on the propagation of a self-sufficient system of human values. But they differ in that they also propose to distinguish the humanities from the social sciences as well as from the physical sciences, and in that they dispute among themselves as to whether an emphasis on the subject matter or on the methods of the humanities is most effectual in accomplishing this distinction.

In the late 19th century the German philosopher Wilhelm Dilthey called the humanities "the spiritual sciences" and "the human sciences" and described them, simply, as those areas of knowledge that lay outside of, and beyond, the subject matter of the physical sciences.

On the other hand, Heinrich Rickert, a turn-of-the-century Neo-Kantian, argued that it is not subject matter but method of investigation that best characterizes the humanities; Rickert contended that whereas the physical sciences aim to move from particular instances to general laws, the human sciences are "idiographic"--they are devoted to the unique value of the particular within its cultural and human contexts and do not seek general laws.

13.4 Ideal type

Ideal type in the social sciences is the mental construct derived from observable reality although not conforming to it in detail because of deliberate simplification and exaggeration. It is not ideal in the sense that it is excellent, nor is it an average; it is, rather, a logical ideal used to order reality by selecting and accentuating certain elements.

The concept of the ideal type was developed by the early-20th-century German sociologist Max Weber, who used it in his historical studies. Some writers confine the use of ideal types to general, supra-historical phenomena (*e.g.,* bureaucracy) that recur in different times and places, although Weber also used them for historically unique occurrences (*e.g.,* his famous Protestant ethic).

Problems in using the ideal type include its tendency to focus attention on extreme, or polar, phenomena, while overlooking the connections between them, and the difficulty of showing how the types and their elements fit into a conception of a total social system.

13.5 Components of propaganda

The contemporary propagandist employing behavioural theory tends to analyze his problem in terms of at least 10 questions:

1. What are the goals of the propaganda? (What changes are to be brought about? In whom? And when?)

2. What are the present and expected conditions in the world social system?

3. What are the present and expected conditions in each of the subsystems of the world social system (such as international regions, nations, lesser territories, interest groups)?

4. Who should distribute the propaganda--the propagandist or his agents?

5. What symbols should be used?

6. What media should be used?

7. Which reactors should the propaganda be aimed at?

8. How can the effects of the propaganda be measured?

9. By what countermeasures can opponents neutralize or suppress the propaganda?

10. How can such countermeasures be measured and dealt with?

In the present state of social science, this 10-part problem can be solved with only moderate confidence with respect to any really major propaganda campaign, even if one has a great deal of money for research. Yet if the propagandist is to proceed as rationally as possible, he needs the best answers that are available.

13.6 Status of contemporary anthropology

It is true that cultural anthropology has not reached a state of complete coherence. This is clear from the persistence of divergent national traditions and from the way in which research can be impregnated with explicit or implicit ideologies.

It is also true that different schools of thought coexist in the same country and that cultural anthropology is not therefore based on a unified body of concepts, whereas a science is defined above all as a homogeneous language for interpreting a specific level of reality. A "science" of culture would seem possible only if anthropologists could free themselves of ethnocentrism and produce concepts and other elements that were universal, objective, and theoretically significant.

The functionalists think they have fulfilled these conditions. The structuralists challenge this and, in their turn, try to fulfil the conditions.

Thus cultural anthropology--as opposed, for example, to linguistics--has developed only very partially a terminology independent of a national or private language.

These limitations are still encountered by most of the social sciences. But cultural anthropology's primary aim--to permit cross-cultural comparability--makes the problem even more serious.

13.7 Methodology of the empirical sciences

The quest for theoretical self-awareness in the empirical sciences has led to interest in methodological and foundational problems as well as to attempts to axiomatise different empirical theories. Moreover, general methodological problems, such as the nature of scientific explanations, have been discussed intensively among philosophers of science. In all of these endeavours, logic plays an important role.

By and large, there are here three different lines of thought: (1) Often, only the simplest parts of logic--*e.g.*, propositional logic--are appealed to (over and above the mere use of logical notation). Sometimes, claims regarding the usefulness of logic in the methodology of the empirical sciences are, in effect, restricted to such rudimentary applications. This restriction is misleading, however, for most of the interesting and promising connections between methodology and logic lie on a higher level, especially in the area of model theory.

In econometrics, for instance, a special case of the logicians' problems of definability plays an important role under the title "identification problem." On a more general level, logicians have been able to clarify the concept of a model as it is used in the empirical sciences.

In addition to those employing simple logic, two other contrasting types of theorists can be distinguished: (2) philosophers of science, who rely mostly on first-order formulations, and (3) methodologists (*e.g.*, Patrick Suppes, a U.S. philosopher and behavioural scientist), who want to use the full power of set theory and of the

mathematics based on it. Both approaches have advantages. Usually realistic axiomatizations and other reconstructions of actual scientific theories are possible only in terms of set theoretical and other strong mathematical conceptualizations (theories conceived of as "set-theoretical predicates"). In spite of the oversimplification that first-order formulations often entail, however, they can yield theoretical insights because first-order logic (including its model theory) is mastered by logicians much more thoroughly than is set theory.

Many empirical sciences, especially the social sciences, use mathematical tools borrowed from probability theory and statistics, together with such outgrowths of these as decision theory, game theory, utility theory, and operations research. A modest but not uninteresting beginning in the study of their foundations has been made in modern inductive logic.

13.8 Freedom

Among the classical problems in the philosophy of religion are those of free will, self-identity, immortality, evil, and suffering. The freedom of the will is a claim for the uniqueness of the subject, known in occasions of activity in which the subject "comes alive" and realizes his subjectivity as that which cannot be reduced to the behaviour patterns and facts--*i.e.,* the objects--of the natural and social sciences.

Such freedom is realized in responding to a situation that has equally come alive objectively to inspire a person and call forth such response. Some claim the predictable character of human behaviour rules out man's freedom; others state that the extent to which human behaviour is unpredictable argues for freedom.

This controversy, however, does not in any way solve the problem of freedom; it only makes evident what kind of problem the problem of freedom is, viz., how far human nature is capable of being analyzed into behavioural terms without any residue.

13.9 Free will

Free will in humans is the power or capacity to choose among alternatives or to act in certain situations independently of natural, social, or divine restraints. Free will is denied by those who espouse any of various forms of determinism. Arguments for free will are based on the subjective experience of freedom, on sentiments of guilt, on revealed religion, and on the universal supposition of responsibility for personal actions that underlies the concepts of law, reward, punishment, and incentive. In theology, the existence of free will must be reconciled with God's omniscience and goodness (in allowing man to choose badly), and with divine grace, which allegedly is necessary for any meritorious act.

A prominent feature of modern Existentialism is the concept of a radical, perpetual, and frequently agonizing freedom of choice. Jean-Paul Sartre, for example, speaks of the individual "condemned to be free" even though his situation may be wholly determined.

13.10 Functionalism

Functionalism in social sciences refers to the theory based on the premise that all aspects of a society--institutions, roles, norms, etc.--serve a purpose and that all are indispensable for the long-term survival of the society. The approach gained prominence in the works of 19th-century sociologists, particularly those who viewed societies as organisms.

The French sociologist Émile Durkheim argued that it was necessary to understand the "needs" of the social organism to which social phenomena correspond. Other writers have used the concept of function to mean the interrelationships of parts within a system, the adaptive aspect of a phenomenon, or its observable consequences. In sociology, functionalism met the need for a method of analysis; in anthropology it provided an alternative to evolutionary theory and trait-diffusion analysis.

A social system is assumed to have a functional unity in which all parts of the system work together with some degree of internal consistency. Functionalism also postulates that all cultural or social phenomena have a positive function and that all are indispensable. Distinctions have been made between manifest functions, those consequences intended and recognized by participants in the system, and latent functions, which are neither intended nor recognized.

The British anthropologist A.R. Radcliffe-Brown explored the theoretical implications of functionalism as a relationship between a social institution and the "necessary conditions of existence" of a social system. He saw the function of a unit as the contribution it makes to the maintenance of a social structure--*i.e.*, the set of relationships among social units.

In an attempt to develop a more dynamic analysis of social systems, the American sociologist Talcott Parsons introduced a structural-functional approach that employs the concept of function as a link between relatively stable structural categories. Any process or set of conditions that does not contribute to the maintenance or development of the system is said to be dysfunctional. In particular, there is a focus on the conditions of stability, integration, and effectiveness of the system.

13.11 Region

Region in the social sciences, a cohesive area that is homogeneous in selected defining criteria and is distinguished from neighbouring areas or regions by those criteria. It is an intellectual construct created by the selection of features relevant to a particular problem and the disregard of other features considered to be irrelevant. A region is distinguished from an area, which is usually a broader concept designating a portion of the surface of the Earth. Area boundaries are arbitrary, established for convenience. Regional boundaries are determined by the homogeneity and cohesiveness of the section.

Regions may be nodal, defined by the organization of activity about some central place (*e.g.*, a town and its hinterland, or tributary area), or uniform, defined by the homogeneous distribution of some phenomena within it (*e.g.*, a tropical rain forest).

Regions may be defined in terms of single or multiple features or in terms that approach the total content of human occupancy of an area. The most common features in social science are ethnic, cultural, or linguistic (Provence), climatic or topographical (the Tennessee Valley), industrial or urban (the Ruhr), economic specialization (the cotton belt of North America), administrative units (standard government regions in Great Britain), and international political areas (the Middle East).

The concept of region is currently used in analysis, planning, and administration of many national and international public programs. Regionalism, or regional consciousness, the ideological correlate of the concept that develops from a sense of identity within the region, is important in many historical, political, and sociological analyses.

13.12 Sanction

Sanction in the social sciences is a reaction (or the threat or promise of a reaction) by members of a social group indicating approval or disapproval of a mode of conduct and serving to enforce behavioural standards of the group. Punishment (negative sanction) and reward (positive sanction) regulate conduct in conformity with social norms (*see* norm). Sanctions may be diffuse--*i.e.*, spontaneous expressions by members of the group acting as individuals--or they may be organized--*i.e.*, actions that follow traditional and recognized procedures. Sanctions therefore include not only the organized punishments of law but also the formal rewards (*e.g.*, honours and titles) and the informal scorn or esteem by members of a community.

In societies without formal legal institutions, such as courts of law, sanctions are often imposed directly by the wronged individual or group. Reaction is in a socially approved manner and in a form considered proportional to the injury. This may include ridiculing, duelling, injuring, seizing of property, or killing the offender or a member of his group. Among the Eskimo, for example, the appropriate punishment for a man who steals another man's wife is to be ridiculed in a nasty song made up by the injured man. Social context, as well as the kind of offence, determines the type of sanction invoked: legal, religious, and moral sanctions can all operate. A breach of norms committed within a kin group may call for religious sanctions, although the same deed involving different kin groups would invoke jural sanctions.

Sanctions, in addition to functioning as a mechanism of social control, also serve to integrate a society, affirming social beliefs and restating their validity when breached.

13.13 Political economy

Political economy is the branch of social science, which later developed into economics, concerned with the raising of revenue by the state and the increase of the state's general resources. The term was introduced about the beginning of the 17th century to describe the study of the problems of the princely states, which at the close of the Middle Ages in Europe replaced the feudal-ecclesiastical political order. Adam Smith, the first to present a comprehensive systematized study, seemed to equate political economy with the treatment of "the nature and causes of the wealth of nations."

After the nationalistic epoch gave way to individualism or liberalism in the late 18th century, the older state-oriented literature came to be called mercantilism. Works in this period, including David Ricardo's *Principles of Political Economy and Taxation* (1817) and John Stuart Mill's *Principles of Political Economy* (1848), gave increased attention to problems of value and distribution.

The term economics replaced political economy in general usage during the 20th century; the change of name accompanied the expansion of the discipline itself, which had become subdivided into a number of specialties.

14. PSYCHOLOGY AS A SOCIAL SCIENCE

14.1 Psychology

Psychology is the scientific discipline that studies mental processes and behaviour in humans and other animals.

Psychology is the science of individual or group behaviour. The word psychology literally means "study of the mind"; the issue of the relationship of mind and body is pervasive in psychology, owing to its derivation from the fields of philosophy and physiology. Psychology is intimately related to the biological and social sciences.

The broad reach of psychology sometimes gives it the appearance of disunity and promotes the lack of a universally accepted theoretical structure. Some of the divisions within psychology are applied fields, while others are more experimental in nature.

The various applied fields include clinical; counselling; industrial, engineering, or personnel; consumer; and environmental. The most important of these specialties, clinical psychology, is concerned with the diagnosis and treatment of mental disorders. Industrial psychology is used in employee selection and related contexts in business and industry.

The broad field known as experimental psychology includes specializations in child, educational, social, developmental, physiological, and comparative psychology. Of these, child psychology applies psychological theory and research methods to children; educational psychology is concerned with learning processes and problems associated with the teaching of students; social psychology is concerned with group dynamics and other aspects of human behaviour in its social and cultural setting; and comparative psychology deals with behaviour as it differs from one species of animal to another.

The issues studied by psychologists cover a wide spectrum, comprising learning, cognition, intelligence, motivation, emotion, perception, personality, mental disorders, and the study of the extent to which individual differences are inherited or are shaped environmentally, known as behaviour genetics.

14.2 Industrial psychology

In the decade after 1910, when the principles of scientific management were being applied wholesale in U.S. industry, union opposition arose.

Though the unions approved more efficient production arising from better machinery and management, they condemned the speedup practice and complained in particular that Taylorism deprived workers of a voice in the conditions and functions of their work. Complaints were also made that the system caused irritability and fatigue along with physiological and neurological damage among workers.

Misuse of the human element in production was causing declines in both quality and productivity. Industrial engineers then faced the problem of motivating the worker so that the combination of human labour and machine technology would achieve its fullest potential. A partial solution came from the social sciences, and, in the process, industrial psychology emerged.

The major premise of this new discipline was that mass production technologies affect the worker both in the immediate job environment and in relations with fellow workers and supervisors. The first important discoveries in the social context of mass production technology resulted from experiments made by the American social scientist Elton Mayo between 1927 and 1932 at the Hawthorne plant of the Western Electric Company, in Cicero, Ill. Mayo, who earlier had studied problems of physical fatigue among textile workers in a Philadelphia plant, was called in to the Hawthorne works, where industrial engineers were considering the potential effect on productivity of changes in illumination.

The investigators chose two groups of employees working under similar conditions to produce the same part; the research plan was to vary the intensity of the light for the test group but to keep it constant for the control group. To Mayo's surprise, the output of both groups rose. Even when the researchers told one group that the light was going to be changed and then did not change it, the workers expressed satisfaction, saying that they liked the "increased" illumination, and productivity continued to rise.

Mayo saw that the significant variable was not physiological but psychological. A second series of experiments was performed, involving the assembly of telephone relays; test and control groups were subjected to changes in wages, rest periods, workweeks, temperature, humidity, and other factors. Output continued to increase no matter how physical conditions were varied; indeed, even when conditions were returned to what they had been before, productivity remained 25 percent above its original value.

Mayo concluded that the reason for this lay in the attitudes of the workers toward their jobs and toward the company. Merely by asking their cooperation in the test, the investigators had stimulated a new attitude among the employees, who now felt themselves part of an important group whose help and advice were being sought by the company. The name Hawthorne effect was given to such beneficial changes in workers' attitudes, and, within a short time, scientific management incorporated these new findings.

Mayo's studies had suggested that consultation, usually in the form of interviews between labour and management, gave workers a sense of belonging to a team. Industrial engineers and sociologists have suggested additional approaches toward improving motivation and productivity. These include job alternation to relieve boredom; job enlargement, or having the worker perform several tasks on a project rather than performing a single operation; and job enrichment, redesigning the job to make it more challenging.

In a sense, Mayo's work made scientific management even more scientific, because he brought the new behavioural sciences, like social psychology, into the problems of organizing work and the labour-management relationship. It encouraged the development of human-factors engineering and ergonomics, disciplines that attempt to design "user-friendly" equipment accommodating itself to the human physiology and nervous system.

For example, the new engineers try to make certain that a worker's equipment is operable with minimum strain, at a comfortable work level, and with controls easy to reach, see, and manipulate. In brief, they attempt to design the machine around the human mind and body.

14.3 Psychology and education

The attempt to apply scientific method to the study of education dates back to the German philosopher Johann Friedrich Herbart, who called for the application of psychology to the art of teaching. But not until the end of the 19th century, when the German psychologist Wilhelm Max Wundt established the first psychological laboratory at the University of Leipzig in 1879, were serious efforts made to separate psychology from philosophy. Wundt's monumental *Principles of Physiological Psychology* (1874) had significant effects on education in the 20th century.

William James, often considered the father of American psychology of education, began about 1874 to lay the groundwork for his psychophysiological laboratory, which was founded officially at Harvard in 1891. In 1878 he established the first course in psychology in the United States and in 1890 published his famous *The Principles of Psychology,* in which he argued that the purpose of education is to organize the child's powers of conduct so as to fit him to his social and physical environment. Interests must be awakened and broadened as the natural starting points of instruction. James's *Principles* and *Talks to Teachers on Psychology* cast aside the older notions of psychology in favour of an essentially behaviourist outlook; they asked the teacher to help educate heroic individuals who would project daring visions of the future and work courageously to realize them.

James's student Edward L. Thorndike is credited with the introduction of modern educational psychology, with the publication of *Educational Psychology* in 1903. Thorndike attempted to apply the methods of exact science to the practice of psychology. James and Thorndike, together with the American philosopher John Dewey, helped to clear away many of the fantastic notions once held about the successive steps involved in the development of mental functions from birth to maturity.

Interest in the work of Sigmund Freud and the psychoanalytic image of the child in the 1920s, as well as attempts to apply psychology to national training and education tasks in the 1940s and '50s, stimulated the development of educational psychology, and the field has become recognized as a major source for educational theory. Eminent researchers in the field have advanced knowledge of behaviour modification, child development, and motivation.

They have studied learning theories ranging from classical and instrumental conditioning and technical models to social theories and open humanistic varieties. Besides the specific applications of measurement, counselling, and clinical psychology, psychology has contributed to education through studies of cognition, information processing, the technology of instruction, and learning styles.

After much controversy about nature versus nurture and about qualitative versus quantitative methods, Jungian, phenomenological, and ethnographic methods have taken their place alongside psychobiological explanations to help educationists understand the place of heredity, general environment, and school in development and learning.

The relationship between educational theory and other fields of study has become increasingly close. Social science may be used to study interactions and speech to discover what is actually happening in a classroom. Philosophy of science has led educational theorists to attempt to understand paradigmatic shifts in knowledge. The critical literature of the 1960s and '70s attacked all institutions as conveyors of the motives and economic interests of the dominant class.

Both social philosophy and critical sociology have continued to elaborate the themes of social control and oppression as embedded in educational institutions. In a world of social as well as intellectual change, there are necessarily new ethical questions, such as those dealing with abortion, biological experimentation, and child rights, which place new demands on education and require new methods of teaching.

15. MODERNIZATION

15.1 The West and the world

It is not fully understood what produced the leap into modernity and why, just as some groups of hunters and gatherers gave rise to agrarian society, some agrarian societies gave rise to industrial society. What is clear is that it took place between the 16th and 18th centuries and that it began in the countries of north-western Europe--especially England, the Netherlands, northern France, and northern Germany.

This could not have been expected. Compared to the Mediterranean, not to mention Arabic and Chinese civilizations, north-western Europe early in the 16th century was backward, technically and culturally. In the 16th and 17th centuries it was still absorbing the commercial and artistic innovations of the Italian city-states of the Renaissance and making piratical raids, where it could, on the wealthy Spanish empire. It seemed an unlikely candidate for future economic leadership of Europe. Yet it was there that the changes took place that propelled those particular societies into the forefront of world development.

15.2 Protestant Reformation

One reason advanced for this is that north-western Europe was the origin and heartland of the Protestant Reformation of the 16th century. In his great work *The Protestant Ethic and the Spirit of Capitalism* (1904), the German sociologist Max Weber suggested that Roman Catholicism and to an even greater extent such Eastern religions as Hinduism and Buddhism were essentially otherworldly religions. They placed doctrinal emphasis on religious contemplation and the life hereafter. Protestantism, on the other hand, was predominantly a "this-worldly" religion. It broke down the distinction between the church and the world, between the monastery and the marketplace.

Every man was a priest; everything he did, at work or at play, he did in the sight of God. Weber sought to show that Protestantism, and especially its Puritan variety, developed a particular type of character that valued frugality and hard work. Protestantism particularly promoted a work ethic. For the Protestant, all work, all occupations, were in a sense a religious vocation. Work was to be pursued with a fitting seriousness and order, in a spirit of rational enterprise that eschewed waste and frivolous adventurism. Such an attitude was admirably suited--though not intentionally--to the development of industrial capitalism.

The Protestant nations, therefore, according to Weber, invented modern capitalism and so launched the world on a course that it still follows. Some later historians have disputed Weber's thesis and have adduced evidence that the early development of capitalism and of industrial organization preceded the rise of Protestantism. In either case, their mutual accommodation remains striking.

In a similarly persuasive way, the rationality of the Protestant work ethic has seemed linked to the development of modern science. This, too, took place largely in North-Western Europe in the course of the 17th century. In no other place, at no other time, was there anything like the scientific revolution of these years in England, France, and the Netherlands.

15.3 Industrial Revolution

It is true that the Industrial Revolution, in its early phases at least, did not depend on the theoretical science of Isaac Newton, Robert Boyle, or others of the period. What was crucial was the rationalist culture and the scientific habits of mind that this culture nurtured. Moreover, the scientific method of observation, hypothesis, experimentation, and verification could be applied not only to nature but also to society.

Eventually, toward the end of the 18th century, what would later be called social science--economics and sociology especially--began to find a place alongside natural science. The scientific outlook--sceptical, autonomous, applying fixed standards of observation to continually changing phenomena, to reach conclusions that were never to be considered more than provisional--became the hallmark of modern society.

15.4 Transoceanic expansion

Already, by the 17th century, Western Europe had embarked on the course of transoceanic expansion that was to become one of its most notable features in the succeeding centuries. The colonization of America, although uneven, added a vast new domain to the West. In wealth, resources, and physical power, the West took a commanding lead over the rest of the world. From the enormous potentialities of science and industry, it acquired a momentum and a dynamism that pointed to a future immeasurably grander than anything previously achieved.

For the first time, moralists and philosophers began to conceive of the possibility that the modern world might come to be the equal and even the superior of the ancient world of Greece and Rome. The idea of progress and, with it, that of modernism was born.

The world was growing in power and enlightenment and, so far as anyone could see, would continue indefinitely to do so. Western society was not merely plunging ahead on its own; it was paving the way for the rest of the world. As Karl Marx said, albeit two centuries later, "The country that is more developed industrially only shows to the less developed the image of its own future."

15.5 Racism

Racism also called RACIALISM is the concept or idea that there is a causal link between inherited physical traits and certain traits of personality, intellect, or culture and, combined with it, the notion that some races are inherently superior to others.

It is difficult to establish the origins of racist thinking, but certainly one of the most influential of such thinkers was the French writer and diplomat Joseph-Arthur, comte de Gobineau , who published his four-volume *Essay on the Inequality of Human Races* in the middle of the 19th century. He taught the superiority of the white race over all others, and, among the whites, of the Aryans as having reached the heights of civilization.

Gobineau's most important follower was Houston Stewart Chamberlain, who published *The Foundations of the 19th Century* in German in 1899. An Englishman by birth, Chamberlain spent most of his life in Germany, where he was so popular with the ruling class that he became known as the kaiser's anthropologist. He, too, insisted on the superiority of the Teutons, whom he characterized physically as being for the most part tall, fair, and dolichocephalic (longheaded), that is to say, corresponding to the Nordic type. Chamberlain regarded the Jews as alien in spirit to the favoured Teutons, although he admitted the difficulty of distinguishing Jews from Germans on the basis of physical characteristics alone.

Although there were many other writers who developed the modern racist position, such as Ludwig Woltmann and H.F.K. Günther in Germany, and Lothrop Stoddard and Madison Grant in the United States, Gobineau and Chamberlain may be regarded as the intellectual forerunners of the racial theories of the German Nazis.

15.6 Nazi approach

Adolf Hitler himself acknowledged his indebtedness to these theorists, particularly to Chamberlain, for giving him the "scientific" basis for this aspect of his political philosophy.

There were, of course, inner contradictions in the Nazi approach--the fact that so many Germans did not look like Nordics and so many Jews did; the alliance with the Japanese, who had consequently to be exempted from the racial restrictions of the Third Reich; and the difficulty of giving any clear meaning to the concepts of German "blood" or "soul," among others--so that facts had to be replaced by mysticism. In spite of these and other deficiencies, racialism was used as a technique which helped to unify the Germans by identifying the "enemy," gave the people a strong sense of ego enhancement and self-confidence, justified economic exploitation and slave labour, obtained support for the war, and convinced the Germans that they never could be defeated.

Racism thus functioned as one of the most effective techniques of Nazi propaganda for achieving and maintaining power over the German people.

15.7 Colonialism

Although colonialism cannot be compared with Nazism in terms of the violence and virulence of the human destruction it involved, it also found in racialism a helpful rationalization for conquest and expansion. When the Spaniards first went to America, several of their apologists (particularly Francisco de Quevedo and Juan Ginés de Sepúlveda) supplied them with the proper excuses for taking the land away from the Indians and for treating them with complete lack of consideration.

They developed the theory that the Indians had an entirely different origin from that of the Spaniards, that they were not human in the same sense, and that there was therefore no need to accord to them the same treatment as to one's fellow human beings. The familiar refrain of the "white man's burden," which was mainly of British manufacture and which found its literary expression in the writings of Thomas Carlyle, James A. Froude, and Charles Kingsley, and most strongly and clearly in those of Rudyard Kipling, made of imperialism a noble activity destined to bring civilization to the benighted members of other "races." Similarly, the French justified the maintenance of their colonial empire on the basis of their *mission civilisatrice,* their duty to bring civilization to the backward peoples of the world.

In all of these colonizing empires, there were undoubtedly many individuals honestly convinced of the nobility of their motives and their enterprise; at the same time, the feelings of racial superiority that accompanied colonialism played an important part in developing resentments among the colonized which even emancipation and independence have not always made it possible to overcome. There has developed in some parts of the world racialism in reverse, a degree of hostility of coloured peoples against whites as whites.

15.8 Emergence of new nations

It remains true that in general, although with certain striking exceptions, the trend has been away from racism. The emergence of new nations, many of them former colonies, has meant that many more nations composed of "coloured peoples" have an independent voice in international affairs that commands a respectful hearing even from previous colonizers.

The recognition that the treatment of ethnic minorities within a country may have important implications for international relations has focussed attention upon the need to improve inter-group relations in general. The works of scientists like Franz Boas in anthropology and Gunnar Myrdal and others in the social sciences helped to destroy much of the mythological thinking associated with race. The trend has been reversed in the Republic of South Africa, where separation of ethnic groups increased from 1948 on.

In the United States, on the other hand, the movement was gradually and progressively in the direction of providing greater equality of opportunity for all ethnic groups. The first dramatic expression of this tendency was furnished by the unanimous decision of the U.S. Supreme Court on May 17, 1954, based in part on social-science research, that the enforced segregation of black schoolchildren in certain states and localities was contrary to the principles of the U.S. Constitution.

16. CONCEPT OF HUMAN NATURE

16.1 Qualities possessed

The concept of human nature is a common part of everyday thought. The ordinary person feels that he comes to know human nature through the character and conduct of the people he meets. Behind what they do he recognizes qualities that often do not surprise him: he forms expectations as to the sort of qualities possessed by other human beings and about the ways they differ from, for example, dogs or horses.

People are proud, sensitive, eager for recognition or admiration, often ambitious, hopeful or despondent, and selfish or capable of self-sacrifice. They take satisfaction in their achievements, have within them something called a conscience, and are loyal or disloyal. Experience in dealing with and observing people gives rise to a conception of a predictable range of conduct; conduct falling outside the range that is considered not to be worthy of a human is frequently regarded as inhuman or bestial whereas that which is exceptional--in that it lives up to standards which most people recognize but few achieve--is regarded as superhuman or saintly.

16.2 Scale of perfection

The common conception of human nature thus implicitly locates man on a scale of perfection, placing him somewhere above most animals but below saints, prophets, or angels. This idea was embodied in the theme, Hellenic in origin, of the Great Chain of Being--a hierarchical order ascending from the most simple and inert to the most complex and active: mineral, vegetable, animal, man, and finally divine beings superior to man. In the Middle Ages these divine beings constituted the various orders of angels, with God as the single, supremely perfect and omnipotent, ever-active being.

There was a tendency in this theory to take for granted the commonality among all human beings, something by virtue of which they could be classified as fully human, which differentiates them from all other animals, and which gives them their place in the order of things. Yet, as with many notions that are habitually employed, the request for a precise definition of "human nature" proves highly problematic.

The Greeks--most notably Plato and Aristotle--introduced the notion of form, nature, or essence as an explanatory, metaphysical concept. Variations on this concept were central to Western thought until the 17th century. Observation of the natural world raised the question of why creatures reproduced after their kind and could not be interbred at will and of why, for example, acorns grew into oaks and not into roses.

16.3 Modern biological concept

To explain such phenomena it was postulated that the seeds, whether plant or animal, must each already contain within them the form, nature, or essence of the species from which they were derived and into which they would subsequently develop. This pattern of explanation is preserved in the modern biological concept of a genetic code that is embodied in the DNA molecular structure of each cell. There are important differences, however, between the modern concept of a genetic code and the older, Greek-derived concept of form or essence.

First, biologists are now able to locate, isolate, experimentally analyze, and manipulate DNA molecules in what has become known as genetic engineering. Being the structures responsible for physical development, DNA molecules represent the terms by which man can be biologically characterized.

Forms or essences, on the other hand, were not observable; if they were granted any independent existence, it was as immaterial entities. The form, nature, or essence of man or of any other kind of being was posited as a principle present in the thing, determining its kind by producing in it an innate tendency to strive to develop into a perfect example of itself--to fulfil its nature and to realize its full potential as a thing of a given kind.

This gave rise to a teleological, or purposive, view of the natural world in which developments were explained by reference to the goal toward which each natural thing, by its nature, strives; *i.e.,* by reference to the ideal form it seeks to realize. By contrast, the genetic structure present in each cell is now invoked to explain the subsequent development of an organism in a "mechanistic" and non-purposive way, in which development is shown to be dependent upon and determined by pre-existing structures and conditions.

Second, genetic mutability forms an essential part of modern evolutionary biology. Not only are there genetic differences between individuals of a given species to account for differences between them in features, such as coloration, but random genetic mutation in the presence of changing environmental conditions may result in alterations to the genetic constitution of the species as a whole.

Thus, in evolutionary biological theory species are not stable; natural kinds do not have the fixed, immutable forms or essences characteristic of biology before the advent of evolutionary theory.

16.4 Role of environment

Within either framework, if human nature is understood simply as man's special form of that which is biologically inherited in all species, there remains the delicate problem of discovering, in any given case, exactly what role environment plays in determining the actual characteristics of mature members of the species.

Even in the case of purely physiological characteristics this may be far from straightforward: for example, the extent to which diet, exercise, and conditions of work determine such things as susceptibility to heart disease and cancer remains the subject of intensive scientific investigation.

16.5 Psychological characteristics

In the case of behavioural and psychological characteristics, such as intelligence, the problems are multiplied to the point where they are no longer problems that can be answered by purely empirical investigation. There is room for much conceptual debate about what is meant by intelligence and over what tests, if any, can be supposed to yield a direct measure of this capacity, and thus provide evidence that an individual's level of intelligence is determined at birth (by nature) rather than by subsequent exposure to the environment (nurture) that conditions the development of all his capacities.

This debate--whether the variation in intelligence levels is a product of the conditions into which people all having the same initial potential are born, or whether it is a reflection of variations in the capacities with which they are born--is very closely related to the question of whether there is such a thing as human nature common to all human beings, or whether there are intrinsic differences among those whom we recognize as belonging to the biological species *Homo sapiens*.

This is because, as the name *Homo sapiens* suggests, man is traditionally thought to be distinguished from and privileged above other animals by virtue of his possession of reason, or intellect. When the intellect is positively valued as that which is distinctively human and which confers superiority on man, the thought that different races of people differ by nature in their intellectual capacities has been used as a justification for a variety of racist attitudes and policies.

Those of another race, of supposedly lesser intellectual development, are classified as less than fully human and therefore as needing to be accorded less than full human rights.

Similarly, the thought that women are by nature intellectually inferior to men has been used as a justification for their domination by men, for refusing them education, and even for according them the legal status of property owned by men.

On the other hand, if differences in adult intellectual capacity are regarded as a product of the circumstances in which potentially similar people are brought up, the attitude is to consider all as equally human but some as having been more privileged when growing up than others.

16.6 Objectivity of standards

More radically, the evidence for variations in intelligence levels may be questioned by challenging the objectivity of the standards relative to which these levels are assessed. It may be argued that conceptions of what constitutes a rational or intelligent response to a situation or to a problem are themselves culturally conditioned, a product of the way in which the members of the group devising the tests and making the judgments have themselves been taught to think.

Such an argument has the effect of undermining claims by any one human group to intellectual superiority over others, whether these others be their contemporaries or their own forebears. Hence, they may also be used to discredit any idea of a progressive development of human intellectual capacities.

These debates about intelligence and rationality provide an example of the complexity of the impact of evolutionary biology on conceptions of human nature, for the dominant traditions in Western thought about human nature have tended to concentrate attention more on what distinguishes man from other animals than on the strictly biological constitution that he largely shares with them. Possession of reason or intellect is far from being the only candidate considered for such a distinguishing characteristic.

Man has been characterized as essentially a tool user, or fabricator (Homo faber), as essentially social, as essentially a language user, and so on. These represent differing views concerning the fundamental feature that gives rise to all the other qualities regarded as distinctively human and which serve to mark man off from other animals. These characteristics all centre on mental, intellectual, psychological--*i.e.*, non-physiological--characteristics and thus leave scope for debate about the relation between mind and body.

So long as this question remains open, and so long as mental or intellectual constitution remains the central consideration in discussions of human nature, the question of changes in--and of the possible evolution of--human nature will remain relatively independent of those devoted to physiological change and hence of strictly biological evolution.

16.7 Renaissance humanists

Until the 15th century the standard assumption was that man had a fixed nature, one that determined both his place in the universe and his destiny. The Renaissance humanists, however, proclaimed that what distinguishes man from all other creatures is that he has no nature. This was a way of asserting that man's actions are not bound by laws of nature in the way that those of other creatures are. Man is capable of taking responsibility for his own actions because he has the freedom to exercise his will. This view received two subsequent interpretations.

First, the human character is indefinitely plastic; each individual is given determinate form by the environment in which he is born, brought up, and lives. In this case, changes or developments in human beings will be regarded as the product of social or cultural changes, changes that themselves are often more rapid than biological evolution. It is thus to disciplines such as history, politics, and sociology, rather than to biology, that one should look for an understanding of these processes.

But if disciplines such as these must constitute the primary study of man, then the question of the extent to which this can be a strictly scientific study arises. The methods of history are not, and cannot be, those of the natural sciences. And the legitimacy of the claims of the so-called social or human sciences to genuine scientific status has frequently been called into question and remains a focus for debate.

Second, each individual is autonomous and must "make" himself. Assertion of the autonomy of man involves rejection of the possibility of discovering laws of human behaviour or of the course of history, for freedom is precisely not being bound by law, by nature. In this case, the study of man can never be parallel to the natural sciences with their theoretical structures based on the discovery of laws of nature.

17. SOCIAL STRUCTURE AND CHANGE

17.1 Ekistics

Ekistics is the science of human settlements. Ekistics involves the descriptive study of all kinds of human settlements and the formulation of general conclusions aimed at achieving harmony between the inhabitants of a settlement and their physical and socio-cultural environments.

Descriptive study involves the examination of the content, such as man alone or in societies, of a settlement, and the settlement container, or the physical settlement, composed of natural and human-made elements.

The examination of settlement content and the physical settlement involves the investigation of five basic elements of human settlement:

1. nature, including physical geography, soil resources, water resources, plant and animal life, and climate;

2. human biological and emotional needs, sensations and perceptions, and moral values;

3. society, including population characteristics, social stratification, cultural patterns, economic development, education, health and welfare, and law and administration;

4. shells, or structures, in which people live and function, such as housing, schools, hospitals, shopping centres and markets, recreational facilities, civic and business centres, and industries;

5. and networks, or systems, that facilitate life and day-to-day functions of inhabitants such as water and power systems, transportation networks, communication systems, and the settlement's physical layout.

17.2 Human settlement

A result of the descriptive study of human settlement and its five basic elements is settlement classification according to the size and number of units which form the settlement; the permanency of the settlement or the degree to which it is continually inhabited; the method by which the settlement was created, such as a settlement that emerged or evolved naturally or one that was preconceived; and the most important form of settlement classification, that according to purpose or function.

The most common functional classifications are rural settlements, institutional settlements established for a specific purpose, and urban settlements.

The descriptive study of human settlements also analyzes the anatomy of the settlement. Settlements or parts of settlements can be classified according to their degree of functional homogeneity, the type and number of central place functions, the circulatory patterns found within the settlement, or any special function or purpose observable in the settlement.

The main purpose or function of a settlement can serve to categorize the settlement as a homogeneous region, such as a single farmstead classified as a homogeneous agricultural region or a bedroom community identified as a homogeneous residential region.

Human settlements can be identified as central places that function as marketplaces, administrative centres, and social and cultural meeting places serving surrounding hinterlands. Circulatory patterns unite settlements by providing transport of people, goods, and information along lines of circulation such as roads.

Nodal regions, or settlements, often form at the intersection of circulatory lines. Unique functions observable within a settlement sometimes are identified as a special settlement area, such as an army camp within a larger residential settlement or a large factory or business in the midst of a relatively homogeneous residential area. Most human settlements possess some form of all these types at some geographic scale.

17.3 Knowledge from other disciplines

Unlike other disciplines or sciences interested primarily in one element of human settlement--such as society (sociology) or shells (architecture or engineering)--ekistic study draws upon the knowledge of economics, social science, technical disciplines, and cultural disciplines.

Two fields of study closely allied to ekistics are urban geography and regional science, but neither claims the comprehensive approach advocated in ekistics.

By drawing from the knowledge of other fields of study in the classification and anatomical study of human settlements, ekistics seeks to draw general conclusions or formulate theories or laws that can be used by builders, planners, architects, engineers, and other creators of human settlements in prescriptive action to cure the maladies of existing settlements and prevent such ills in future settlements.

17.4 Economic and social structure

Industrialism, at least within our experience of it for more than 200 years, never reaches a point of equilibrium or a level plateau. By its very principle of operation, it ceaselessly innovates and changes. Having largely eliminated the agricultural work force, it moves on manufacturing employment by creating new automated technology that increases manufacturing productivity while displacing workers.

Manufacturing, from accounting for a half or more of the employed population of industrial societies, shrinks to between a quarter and a third. Its place is filled by the service sector, which in fully industrial societies comes to employ between a half and two-thirds of the work force and to account for more than half of the gross national product. Most service occupations--in government, health, education, finance, leisure and entertainment--are white-collar.

The typical industrial worker is now not the blue-collar worker but the white-collar worker.

The move to a service society is marked by a great expansion in education, health, and other private and public welfare services. The population typically becomes not just healthier, better housed, and better fed but also better educated.

17.5 Marketable commodity

Most young people complete secondary- or high-school education; between a quarter and a half of them go on to full-time higher education. Professional and scientific knowledge becomes the most marketable commodity.

The "knowledge class" of professional, scientific, and technical workers becomes the fastest-growing occupational group. The link between pure science and technology, loose and uncertain in the early stages of industrialization, becomes pivotal. New industries, starting with chemicals and pharmaceuticals and later including the aeronautical, space, and nuclear industries, are created by developments in pure science and depend largely on theoretical research.

Theoretical knowledge in the social sciences also comes to be widely applied, as in Keynesian management of the national economy and in complex models of technological and economic forecasting.

18. POST-MODERN OR POST-INDUSTRIAL SOCIETY

18.1 Changes compared with classic forms

Struck by these changes, as compared with the classic forms of industrial society of the 19th and early 20th centuries, some theorists, notably the American sociologist Daniel Bell, have discerned a movement to a new post-modern or post-industrial society. Such conclusions may be premature.

Most of the changes characterizing late industrialism can be seen as the results of long-term developments implicit in the process of industrialization from the start. The rise of service industries has emerged in part from the increase in leisure and in disposable wealth and in part from the continuing process of mechanization and technical innovation, which constantly raises manufacturing productivity by replacing human labour with machines.

It can also be seen as the consequence of the growth of multinational corporations; this, too, is the result of the increase in scale and complexity of industrial organization, a clear tendency from the very start. The growth of knowledge-based industries, finally, represents no break with the past. Science has always been at the base of industrialism and its closer union with industry and society in the 20th century is simply the fulfilment of modernization's rationalizing drive.

18.2 Emergence of new values and problems

But, while there may be no new society, these changes do add a new dimension to modern societies. Beyond a certain point in economic development, new values and problems emerge. The activities of the multinationals seem to encourage a process of "de-industrialization" in many modern societies, a drastic decline in manufacturing output and employment as these functions shift to the Third World.

While services have for the time being filled the breach, it cannot be assumed that such a balancing will continue, at least as far as employment is concerned.

18.3 Applications of computers

The new microelectronic technology, itself simply the latest wave of industrial tools, has made inroads into service employment faster than more traditional industrial machines displaced manufacturing workers.

The application of computers to information processing in a wide range of service work may threaten in turn to displace the vast mass of routine white-collar workers. Nor are the jobs of the more skilled workers necessarily much safer: Computer-aided design may take over much of the draftsman's and architect's work as computer-aided manufacturing equipment displaces skilled machinists; electronic audiovisual equipment may to a large extent take the place of the classroom teacher; and self-service diagnostic software may eliminate many tasks of the nurse and doctor.

18.4 Science fiction

Science fiction is a form of fiction that developed in the 20th century and deals principally with the impact of actual or imagined science upon society or individuals. The term is more generally used to refer to any literary fantasy that includes a scientific factor as an essential orienting component.

Such literature may consist of a careful and informed extrapolation of scientific facts and principles, or it may range into far-fetched areas flatly contradictory of such facts and principles. In either case, plausibility based on science is a requisite, so that such precursors of the genre as Mary Shelley's Gothic novel *Frankenstein, or the Modern Prometheus* (1818) and Robert Louis Stevenson's *Strange Case of Dr. Jekyll and Mr. Hyde* (1886) are science fiction, whereas Bram Stoker's *Dracula* (1897), based as it is purely on the supernatural, is not.

Science fiction was made possible only by the rise of modern science itself, notably the revolutions in astronomy and physics. Aside from the age-old genre of fantasy literature, which does not qualify, there were notable precursors: imaginary voyages to the moon or to other planets in the 18th century and space travel in Voltaire's *Micromégas* (1752), alien cultures in Jonathan Swift's *Gulliver's Travels* (1726), and science-fiction elements in the 19th-century stories of Edgar Allan Poe, Nathaniel Hawthorne, and Fitz-James O'Brien. Science fiction proper began, however, toward the end of the 19th century with the scientific romances of Jules Verne, whose science was rather on the level of invention, as well as the science-oriented novels of social criticism by H.G. Wells.

18.5 Development of science fiction

The development of science fiction as a self-conscious genre dates from 1926 when Hugo Gernsback, who coined the portmanteau word scientifiction, founded *Amazing Stories* magazine, which was devoted exclusively to science-fiction stories. Published in this and other pulp magazines with great and growing success, such stories were not viewed as serious literature but as sensationalism. With the advent in 1937 of a demanding editor, John W. Campbell, Jr., of *Astounding Science Fiction* (founded in 1930) and with the publication of stories and novels by such writers as Isaac Asimov, Arthur C. Clarke, and Robert A. Heinlein, science fiction emerged as a mode of serious fiction. Ventures into the genre by writers who were not devoted exclusively to science fiction, such as Aldous Huxley, C.S. Lewis, and Kurt Vonnegut, also added respectability.

A great boom in the popularity of science fiction followed World War II. The increasing intellectual sophistication of the genre and the emphasis on wider societal and psychological issues significantly broadened the appeal of science fiction to the reading public. Science fiction became international, extending into the Soviet Union and other eastern European nations.

Serious criticism of the genre became common, and, in the United States particularly, science fiction was studied as literature in colleges and universities. Magazines arose that were dedicated to informing the science-fiction fan on all aspects of the genre. Some science-fiction works became paperback best-sellers.

Besides such acknowledged masters of the genre as Clarke, Heinlein, and Asimov, science-fiction writers of notable merit in the post-war period included A.E. Van Vogt, J.G. Ballard, Ray Bradbury, Frank Herbert, Harlan Ellison, Poul Anderson, Samuel R. Delany, Ursula K. LeGuin, Frederik Pohl, Octavia E. Butler, and Brian Aldiss.

These writers' approaches included predictions of future societies on Earth, analyses of the consequences of interstellar travel, and imaginative explorations of forms of intelligent life and their societies in other worlds. Radio, television, and motion pictures have reinforced the popularity of the genre.

18.6 Conclusion on social structure

Social structure and social change are central theoretical concepts of the social sciences that refer to basic and complementary characteristics of social life in general--permanence, continuity, and repetitiveness on the one hand, dynamics and changeability on the other.

Both concepts are interconnected: the social structure cannot be conceptualized adequately without some notion of actual or potential change, and social change as a more or less regular process is inconceivable without the notion of continuity. To the degree that change processes are regular and interconnected, social change itself is structured.

Any separation of the two concepts, as though they refer to divergent fields, is therefore misleading. This is not to deny that the relative stress on either structural continuity or dynamic change varies in social scientific theories and empirical studies. Since about 1965 there has been a shift from "structure" to "change" in social theory.

Change on different levels (social dynamics in everyday life, short-term transformations and long-term developments in society at large) has become the focus of attention.

END

19. BIBLIOGRAPHY

1. MORAL PHILOSOPHY, FROM SOCRATES TO THE 21ST AEON, ISBN: 978-1-4457-4618-0
2. MORAL PHILOSOPHY, FROM HIPPOCRATES TO THE 21ST AEON, ISBN: 978-1-84753-463-7
3. THERAPEUTIC PHILOSOPHY FOR THE INDIVIDUAL AND THE STATE, ISBN: 978-1-4092-7586-2
4. PHILOSOPHIC COUNSELLING FOR PEOPLE AND THEIR GOVERNMENTS, ISBN: 978-1-4092-7400-1
5. MORAL PHILOSOPHY, THE ETHICAL APPROACH THROUGH THE AGES, ISBN: 978-1-4092-7703-3
6. MORAL PHILOSOPHY, ISBN: 978-1-4478-5037-3
7. PSYCHOANALYSIS, POETRY, ISBN: 978-1-4467-2741-6
8. PLATO'S EPISTEMOLOGY, ISBN: 978-1-4716-6584-4
9. ARISTOTLE'S AETIOLOGY, ISBN: 978-1-4716-7861-5
10. MARXISM, SOCIALISM & COMMUNISM, ISBN: 978-1-4716-8236-0
11. MACHIAVELLI'S POLITICS & RELEVANT PHILOSOPHICAL CONCEPTS, ISBN: 978-1-4716-8629-0
12. BRITISH PHILOSOPHERS, 16TH TO 18TH CENTURY, ISBN: 978-1-4717-1072-8
13. ROUSSEAU ON WILL AND MORALITY, ISBN: 978-1-4717-1070-4
14. HEGEL ON IDEALISM, KNOWLEDGE & REALITY, ISBN: 978-1-4717-0954-8
15. PHILOLOGY, CONCEPTS OF EUROPEAN LITERATURE, ISBN: 978-1-291-49148-7
16. THREE MILLENNIA OF HELLENIC PHILOLOGY, ISBN: 978-1291-49799-1
17. CYPRUS, PERMANENT DEPRIVATION OF FREEDOM, ISBN: 978-1-291-50833-8
18. MEDICAL ETHICS THROUGH THE AGES, ISBN: 978-1-4092- 7468-1
19. MEDICAL ETHICS, FROM HIPPOCRATES TO THE 21ST CENTURY ISBN: 978-1-4457-1203-1
20. THE MISINTERPRETATION OF SIGMUND FREUD, ISBN: 978-1-4467-1659-5
21. JUNG'S PSYCHOTHERAPY: THE PSYCHOLOGICAL & MYTHOLOGICAL METHODS, ISBN: 978-1-4477-4740-6
22. FREUDIAN ANALYSIS & JUNGIAN SYNTHESIS, ISBN: 978-1-4477-5996-6
23. PSYCHOLOGY FROM CONCEPTION TO SENILITY, ISBN: 978-1-4092-7218-2
24. PSYCHOTHERAPY, CONCEPTS OF TREATMENT, ISBN: 978-1-291-50178-0
25. PSYCHOLOGY, CONCEPTS OF BEHAVIOUR, ISBN: 978-1-291-47573-9
26. PSYCHOLOGY OF CHILD CULTURE, ISBN: 978-1-4092-7619-7
27. JOYFUL PARENTING, ISBN: 0 9527956 1 2
28. THE GUIDE TO A JOYFUL PARENTING, ISBN: 0 952 7956 1 2
29. PHILOSOPHY FOR HUMAN BEHAVIOUR, ISBN: 978-1-291-12707-2
30. SOCIOLOGY, CONCEPTS OF GROUP BEHAVIOUR, ISBN: 978-1-291-51888-7
31. SOCIAL SCIENCES, CONCEPTS OF BRANCHES AND RELATIONSHIPS, ISBN: 978-1-291-52321-8